014600009 Liverpool Univ

KU-442-044

Understanding CELEBRITY

University of Liverpool

Withdrawn from stock

SAGE has been part of the global academic community since 1965, supporting high quality research and learning that transforms society and our understanding of individuals, groups and cultures. SAGE is the independent, innovative, natural home for authors, editors and societies who share our commitment and passion for the social sciences.

Find out more at: **www.sagepublications.com**

Understanding CELEBRITY

GRAEME TURNER

SECOND
EDITION

Los Angeles | London | New Delhi
Singapore | Washington DC

Los Angeles | London | New Delhi
Singapore | Washington DC

SAGE Publications Ltd
1 Oliver's Yard
55 City Road
London EC1Y 1SP

SAGE Publications Inc.
2455 Teller Road
Thousand Oaks, California 91320

SAGE Publications India Pvt Ltd
B 1/I 1 Mohan Cooperative Industrial Area
Mathura Road
New Delhi 110 044

SAGE Publications Asia-Pacific Pte Ltd
3 Church Street
#10-04 Samsung Hub
Singapore 049483

Editor: Mila Steele
Editorial Assistant: James Piper
Production editor: Imogen Roome
Copyeditor: Audrey Scriven
Proofreader: Kate Harrison
Marketing manager: Michael Ainsley
Cover design: Jen Crisp
Typeset by: C&M Digitals (P) Ltd, Chennai, India
Printed and bound by CPI Group (UK) Ltd,
Croydon, CR0 4YY

© Graeme Turner 2014

First edition published 2004. Reprinted 2007, 2008, 2009
(twice), 2010 and 2012

Apart from any fair dealing for the purposes of research or
private study, or criticism or review, as permitted under the
Copyright, Designs and Patents Act, 1988, this publication
may be reproduced, stored or transmitted in any form, or
by any means, only with the prior permission in writing of
the publishers, or in the case of reprographic reproduction,
in accordance with the terms of licences issued by the
Copyright Licensing Agency. Enquiries concerning
reproduction outside those terms should be sent to the
publishers.

Library of Congress Control Number: 2013935373

British Library Cataloguing in Publication data

A catalogue record for this book is available from
the British Library

MIX
Paper from
responsible sources
FSC
www.fsc.org   FSC® C013604

ISBN 978-1-4462-5320-5
ISBN 978-1-4462-5321-2 (Pbk)

Contents

Acknowledgment

I wish to acknowledge the contributions made to this project by my collaborators on an earlier, Australian, book on celebrity (*Fame Games: The Production of Celebrity in Australia*, 2000): Frances Bonner and P. David Marshall. I learnt a great deal from them over the course of writing that book, and much of what I learnt from them has helped me immeasurably in writing this one. Of course, in what follows I directly acknowledge their published work, but this is to recognise also that their contribution has been at a more informal and collegial level as well – conversations, advice, references, and the odd raised eyebrow, they have all helped.

I would also like to thank a number of colleagues who have read drafts of this material and provided me with comments. Frances Bonner, in particular, read the whole thing with her customary generosity, while John Hartley and Alan McKee read less but were also generous and thoughtful in their comments. The project itself was initiated at the invitation of Julia Hall from Sage during a research seminar at the Media and Cultural Studies Centre at the University of Sunderland, where I was a visiting professor from 2000–2003. I would like to thank John Storey and his colleagues (in particular Angie Werndly and Andy Crisell) for inviting me into their professional lives and for making me so welcome there. For her comments during that seminar, which she probably no longer remembers but which proved to be useful, I would like to thank Joke Hermes. Three of my graduate students have worked as research assistants for me at various stages, so my thanks go to Susan Luckman, John Gunders and Elizabeth Tomlinson. My colleagues at the Centre for Critical and Cultural Studies at the University of Queensland have provided me with the very best environment to do my work, and the Centre's Project Officer, Andrea Mitchell, has been assiduous in protecting my time as well as running the centre like a well oiled machine. Finally, I would like to thank my wife, Chris, for her love and support.

Acknowledgment to the Second Edition

For this second edition I wish to acknowledge the contribution to my work on celebrity in general, and to this book in particular, from my colleague in the Centre for Critical and Cultural Studies, Anthea Taylor, who has commented helpfully on some of the revised material, and with whom I have had so many productive conversations over the last four years. I also wish to acknowledge the organisers of the inaugural international Celebrity Studies conference at Deakin University, Melbourne, in 2012, James Bennett and Sean Redmond; I have drawn on the material presented there in the concluding chapter. Finally, my thanks go to Mila Steele of Sage who gently coerced me into undertaking this updated version of *Understanding Celebrity*; I hope it has turned out the way she had hoped.

Preface

What is left to say about celebrity? Well, as I hope to demonstrate in this book, quite a lot. In particular, I have been concerned to disaggregate the customary constructions of celebrity a little, recognising celebrity's multiple industrial locations, for instance, so that we maintain a sense of the difference between the varieties of fame produced by the film industry, television, sports, the business world and so on. Also, I have been conscious that the dominant pattern within cultural studies' discussion of celebrity has been to concentrate on 'celebrity culture', effectively defined as a field of representation. The analysis of the specific celebrity as a text – mostly historicised and contextualised but sometimes not – remains the dominant paradigm within cultural and media studies approaches to understanding celebrity. In this book, I have explored alternatives to this paradigm by devoting a significant proportion of the analysis to the industry that produces these celebrity texts and to the processes that structure their consumption.

Consequently, I have divided this book into three parts. In **Part One: Introduction,** I begin by presenting an overview of the history of celebrity and its analysis, directed towards a preliminary understanding of the cultural function of celebrity. In **Part Two: Production,** I discuss the promotions and publicity industries that produce celebrity before examining the contemporary trend in television where the manufacture of celebrity has been closely articulated to the generation of new formats and products. In **Part Three: Consumption,** I focus on the modes and purposes of the consumption of celebrity, ranging from the public reaction to the death of Diana, Princess of Wales, to the attractions provided by celebrity websites. The cultural functions served by celebrity emerge as highly varied and contingent, challenging any simple definition of what might constitute a celebrity culture. Structuring the book in this way has enabled me to give equal (well, almost equal) attention to the discursive constitution of celebrity (its ambivalence, the role played by the signs of authenticity, for instance); to the industrial structures that produce and distribute it; and to the cultural processes through which it is consumed. In my view, that gives us at least a starting point from which we might begin to properly understand celebrity as it operates in contemporary culture.

Graeme Turner, Brisbane, July 2003

Preface to the Second Edition

The first edition of this book was written a decade ago, and much has changed since then. In particular, the production and consumption of celebrity online has become a fundamental, indeed a mainstream, activity. While the first edition dealt with those aspects of the online environment that were around at the time, there are important platforms which have appeared since then which demand attention: the use of Twitter, to name but one, has transformed the celebrity-fan relation as well as troubling many of the systems of industrial control used to manage the production of celebrity. In order to maintain the structure of the book – the division between production and consumption, aimed at giving both their due – I have resisted the temptation (and some suggestions) that I write a new chapter about celebrity and new media. I have preferred to insert material on new media, digital media, or mobile media as I go, integrating it into the larger arguments I have made in order to update them. Inevitably this complicates them as well; once you introduce social media into the picture, for instance, that ushers in a whole lot of issues about what counts as mass media, and about the importance of scale in such a calculation.

While most of the additional material deals with the changes associated with new media platforms, this new edition is also a thorough revision of the earlier version: some material has been added, some removed, and the orientation of the overall argument has shifted slightly to reflect important shifts in the field of celebrity studies. While the first edition was primarily concerned with establishing the need for media and cultural scholars to consider celebrity as an industry as well as a field of representations, some of the changes in this edition reflect a growing concern, within celebrity studies itself, with better understanding the cultural and political consequences of celebrity's prominence in our media culture. The result, I hope, is a significant updating of the arguments, the media platforms discussed, and the examples used, which will extend and enhance the usefulness of this book.

Graeme Turner, Brisbane, February 2013

Part one

Introduction

1 | Understanding Celebrity

The familiar stranger is by no means unprecedented in history. People have long imagined a world populated by figures who were not physically at hand and yet seemed somehow present. What has changed, of course, is the magnitude of the flow, the range of characters that enter our world, their omnipresence, the sheer number of stories. Inevitably, today's stories are but prologues or sequels to other stories, true and less true stories, stories that are themselves intermissions, stories without end. (Gitlin, 2001: 22)

CELEBRITY TODAY

What are the conditions of celebrity today? The contemporary celebrity will usually have emerged from the sports or entertainment industries, they will be highly visible through the media, and their private life will attract greater public interest than their professional life. Unlike that of, say, public officials, the celebrity's fame does not necessarily depend on the position or achievements that gave them their prominence in the first instance. Rather, once they are established, their fame is likely to have outstripped the claims to prominence developed within that initial location. Indeed, the modern celebrity may claim no special achievements other than the attraction of public attention; think, for instance, of the prominence gained for short, intense periods by the contestants on *Big Brother* or *Survivor*, or even the more sustained public visibility of Kim Kardashian. As a result, and as the example of Kim Kardashian might suggest, most media pundits would argue that celebrities in the twenty-first century excite a level of public interest that seems, for one reason or another, disproportionate. While those who have studied this phenomenon might well argue that this excessiveness constitutes an intrinsic element of the celebrity's appeal, it is also one reason why celebrity is so often regarded as the epitome of the inauthenticity or constructedness of mass-mediated popular culture (Franklin, 1997).

As the epigraph at the top of this chapter suggests, it is the pervasiveness of celebrity across the modern mass media that encourages us to think of it as a new development, rather than simply the extension of a long-standing condition. The exorbitance of celebrity's contemporary cultural visibility is unprecedented, and the role that the celebrity plays across many aspects of the cultural field has certainly expanded and multiplied in recent years. We are still debating, however, what constitutes celebrity – how precisely to describe and understand this phenomenon. Properly assessing the scale and provenance of celebrity – as a discursive category, as a commercial commodity, as the object of consumption – is a process that is now well under way, but there are still many definitional issues to be clarified. In this chapter, I want to continue this process through a discussion of some key debates: around the definitions and taxonomies of celebrity; the history of the production of celebrity; and the social function of celebrity.

WHAT IS CELEBRITY?

Let's consider some options. First, commentary in the popular media by columnists and other public intellectuals tends to regard the modern celebrity as a symptom of a worrying cultural shift: towards a culture that privileges the momentary, the visual and the sensational over the enduring, the written, and the rational.[1] Second, those who consume and invest in celebrity tend to describe it as an innate or 'natural' quality, which is possessed only by some extraordinary individuals and 'discovered' by industry talent scouts. For the popular press, the fanzines, the television and movie industries, the defining qualities of the celebrity are both natural and magical: journalists, feature writers and publicists speak of their 'presence', their 'star quality', and their 'charisma'. Third, and in striking contrast to this, the academic literature, particularly from within cultural and media studies, has tended to focus on celebrity as the product of a number of cultural and economic processes. These include the commodification of the individual celebrity through promotion, publicity and advertising; the implication of celebrities in the processes through which cultural identity is negotiated and formed; and most importantly, the representational strategies employed by the media in their treatment of prominent individuals. The sum of these processes constitutes a celebrity *industry*, and it is important that cultural studies' accounts of celebrity deal with its production as a fundamental structural component of how the media operate at the moment. In this section, I want to touch on aspects of these broad approaches to the nature and function of celebrity.

Daniel Boorstin is responsible for one of the most widely quoted aphorisms about celebrity: 'the celebrity is a person who is well-known for their well-knownness' (1971: 58). 'Fabricated on purpose to satisfy our exaggerated expectations of human greatness', says Boorstin, the celebrity develops their capacity for fame, not by achieving great things, but by differentiating their own personality from those of their competitors in the public arena. Consequently, while heroic figures are distinguished by their achievements or by 'the great simple virtues of their character', celebrities are differentiated 'mainly by trivia of personality'. It is not surprising to Boorstin, therefore, that entertainers dominate the ranks of celebrity 'because they are skilled in the marginal differentiation of their personalities' (ibid.: 65).

Boorstin's account was enclosed within a critique that accused contemporary American culture (the first edition was published in 1961) of a fundamental inauthenticity, as it was increasingly dominated by the media's presentation of what he calls the 'pseudo event'. This is an event planned and staged entirely for the media, which accrues significance through the scale of its media coverage rather than through any more disinterested assessment of its importance. The celebrity, in turn, is its human equivalent: the 'human pseudo event', fabricated for the media and evaluated in terms of the scale and effectiveness of their media visibility (ibid.: 57).

Drawing such a close relationship between the celebrity and the inauthenticity of contemporary popular culture interprets celebrity as a symptom of cultural change. Preceding arguments about postmodernity by several decades, but driven by the opposite of postmodernism's reputed relativism, Boorstin describes a culture impelled by its fascination with the image, the simulation, and losing its grounding in substance or reality. While this concern is clearly genuine and shared by many, one has to recognise that elite critiques of movements in popular culture have taken this kind of stand from the beginning. Each new shift in fashion is offered as the end of civilisation as we know it, with the underlying motivation being an elitist distaste for the demotic or populist dimension of mass cultural practices. So, there is a limit to how helpful this is to those who might want to understand popular cultural forms and practices. John Storey reminded me, in his preface to *Inventing Popular Culture*, of Raymond Williams' comment in *Culture and Society* that 'we live in an expanding culture, yet we spend much of our energy regretting the fact, rather than seeking to understand its nature and conditions' (Storey, 2003: xii). That seems to be an accurate reflection on the weakness of the tradition of commentary and analysis I have used Boorstin to represent, and the importance of investigating alternatives.

Boorstin's is far from the only position, of course, from which we might read the modern celebrity as representative of a significant shift in contemporary popular culture. There is the more disinterested and less moralistic proposition that the modern phenomenon of celebrity reflects an ontological shift in popular culture. This constitutes a change in the way cultural meanings are generated as the celebrity becomes a key site of media attention and personal aspiration, as well as one of the key places where cultural meanings are negotiated and organised (Marshall, 1997: 72–3). In the more sociological accounts, this shift is evaluated in terms of a net cultural loss – customarily, a loss of community as human relations attenuate and fragment under the pressure of contemporary political and social conditions. As a result of such conditions, the argument goes, there is an affective deficit in modern life. Some of our closest social relations seem to be in decline: the nuclear family, the extended family and the withdrawal of the family unit from the wider suburban community, are among the symptoms we might name. The diminution of direct social relations is addressed by what has been called para-social interactions (that is, interactions which occur across a significant social distance – with people 'we don't know'), such as those we enjoy with the celebrities we watch and admire (Rojek, 2001: 52). Among our compensations for the loss of community is an avid attention to the figure of the celebrity and a greater investment in our relations with specific versions of this figure. In effect, we are using celebrity as a means of constructing a new dimension of community through the media.

Both Chris Rojek (2001; 2012) and John Frow (1998) suggest that the cultural function of the celebrity today contains significant parallels with the functions normally ascribed to religion. ('Is Elvis a god?' asks Frow, and on many of the criteria that he lists the answer has to be 'Yes'.) Both have elaborated quite detailed comparisons of the qualities attributed to particular celebrities and to religious figures, as well as of the kinds of spiritual experiences provided for audiences of fans on the one hand and congregations of believers on the other. In his most recent book, Rojek links 'the commodified magnetism' that celebrities possess with a performance culture that routinely 'trades in motifs of unity, ecstasy and transcendence'. In general, he argues in *Fame Attack*, 'religiosity permeates the production, exchange and consumption of celebrity culture' (2012: 121).

Viewed from such a perspective, the attributes of celebrity are held to be imminent in the individual concerned: Elvis's celebrity, in such a context, is the popular recognition of the inherent qualities of this extraordinary individual. Here the discourses of religion seem to coincide with those of the media industries that produce celebrity. The popular view that celebrity is a natural, immanent quality to which the media industries give expression obviously legitimates the interests of the industries concerned as well as consoling those who consume their products as objects of belief, desire or aspiration. And yet, it is important to recognise that such a definition of celebrity is countervailed by equally popular media discourses that empha-sise its phoniness and constructedness. While many stories of individual success might suggest that the individual's 'star quality' has shone through, many others will insist that their achievements are simply the effect of blind good luck, and that 'star quality' has little to do with it. The appeal of such stories explicitly does not lie in the reader's admiration or respect for the celebrity figure or for the process that produces them.[2]

It is increasingly clear that it is the detail that matters as we develop an understanding of the roles played by celebrities within popular culture. Richard Dyer's work (1979; 1986) has been highly influential as a result of his close attention to the detail of the film star as a cultural text, and his concern with contextualising these texts within the discursive and ideologi-cal conditions that have enabled the specific star's ascendancy. Dyer describes the film stars he examines as socially grounded, overdetermined by the historical conditions within which they are produced; conversely, he also gives due weight to the contingency and specificity of the meanings generated by the particular star in relation to their audiences. Dyer's description of the semiotics of film stars found that their social meanings were not only deposited there by repeated representations and perfor-mances, but that they were also the product of complex relations between the kind of individuality the star signified and that valued (or, alternatively, problematised) by the society. As a result, the story Dyer tells about the meanings embedded in the image of Marilyn Monroe is not only a story of the professional cultivation of her persona as a star, but also of the discur-sive and ideological context within which that persona could develop.

Probably the next conceptual shift in the development of definitions of celebrity, and one which moves us a little closer to the contexts of its pro-duction, comes from Joshua Gamson's *Claims to Fame* (1994). Gamson's work is most significant for its focus on the workings of the industries that churn these products out, and for what he is able to tell us about the specific meanings and pleasures derived from them by particular groups of fans and their audiences. There is a wealth of empirical detail in his book too, of which we will be making more use in later chapters.

There was an increased concentration of interest in defining celebrity over the late 1990s and early 2000s, focused around a number of books which have been important in setting the terms for a celebrity studies that differentiated itself from the studies of the film star – that is, the kind of celebrity studies we most commonly see now. *Celebrity and Power* (Marshall, 1997), *Illusions of Immortality* (Giles, 2000), *Fame Games* (Turner, Bonner and Marshall, 2000) and *Celebrity* (Rojek, 2001) are among them. The common tactic here was to emphasise that celebrity is not 'a property of specific individuals. Rather, it is constituted discursively, by the way in which the individual is represented' (Turner et al., 2000: 11). For Rojek, celebrity is the consequence of the 'attribution' of qualities to a particular individual through the mass media (Rojek, 2001: 10), while for David Giles, fame is a 'process', a consequence of the way individuals are treated by the media:

> The brutal reality of the modern age is that all famous people are treated like celebrities by the mass media, whether they be a great political figure, a worthy campaigner, an artist 'touched by genius', a serial killer or Maureen of *Driving School* [one of the participants in a British reality TV program]. The newspapers and television programs responsible for their publicity do not draw any meaningful distinction between *how* they are publicised. (2000: 5)

While we might protest that meaningful distinctions do remain – between, for instance, how stardom is constructed in the cinema, or how we understand the television personality (Bennett, 2011), or the notoriety of the serial killer (Schmid, 2006) – the general point that Giles is making seems to be a fair one. Politicians, television performers, pop stars and the latest evictee from the *Big Brother* house, all seem to be integrated into more or less the same 'publicity regimes and fame-making apparatus' (Langer, 1998: 53). Modern celebrity, then, is overwhelmingly a product of media representation; understanding it demands giving close attention to the representational repertoires and patterns employed in this discursive regime.

In practice, the discursive regime of celebrity is defined by a number of elements. It crosses the boundary between the public and the private worlds, preferring the personal, the private or 'veridical' self (Rojek, 2001: 11) as the privileged object of revelation. We can map the precise moment a public figure becomes a celebrity. It occurs at the point at which media interest in their activities is transferred from reporting on their public role (such as their specific achievement in politics or sport) to investigating the details of their private lives. Paradoxically, it is often the high profile achieved by their public activities that provides the alibi for this process of 'celebritisation'. Conversely, the celebrity's general claim on public attention can easily outstrip the public awareness of their original achievements. Hence we can have a journalist-cum-talk-show host such as Geraldo Rivera who is 'famous for who they are instead of what they report' (Shepard, 1999: 82), or an actor such as Lindsay Lohan whose mediatised notoriety is now out of all proportion to her professional achievements. Longstanding celebrities (even highly successful film stars such as Jack Nicholson) can outlive the memory of their original claims to fame as being famous becomes a career in itself.

None of this is simple, of course. The discourses in play within the media representation of celebrity are highly contradictory and ambivalent: celebrities are extraordinary or they are 'just like us'; they deserve their success or they 'just got lucky'; they are objects of desire and emulation, or they are provocations for derision and contempt; they are genuine down-to-earth people or they are complete phonies (or, in the case of Michael Jackson towards the end of his life, just plain 'wacko'). The territories of desire explored by the representation of celebrities are complex, too. Our fascination with particular celebrities is on the one hand a fantastic projection, but on the other hand we *can* actually encounter them in everyday life. Gamson's descriptions of the fans queuing up to watch celebrities arrive at red-carpet events, and Rojek's discussion of the disruptive effect of the 'out-of-face' encounter (when we accidentally meet a celebrity in *their* everyday life, doing the shopping or crossing the street), suggest how these encounters with the object of one's fantasy can inject significance, even desire, into our own everyday lives. As we will see in Chapter 3, this possibility is now dramatically enhanced by the capacities of social media, where the fan can indeed communicate directly with their favourite celebrity via, for instance, Twitter.

There is one point that largely gets lost in most discussions of celebrity, however. While it is reasonable to think of the discursive regime within which celebrity is represented as more or less the same across the range of media, it is necessary to recognise that the pleasures and identifications on offer to consumers of certain media products can vary markedly. The shock at Princess Diana's death may well stem from an affection that is not dissimilar to that which we might feel for an actual acquaintance, and constitutes a form of empathic identification. The fascination with nude celebrities, exploited by such magazines as *Celebrity Flesh* or such websites as *Hollywood Whores*, is not like that at all. Sitting uncomfortably close to the porn sites merely one click away, the nude celebrity websites have rarely been the subject of any discussion or inquiry (although see Knee, 2006); the overwhelmingly gendered, and often misogynistic, character of this domain of celebrity demands more attention. (There is some discussion of this in Chapter 6.)

Of course, it is important to emphasise how sophisticated the media's production of celebrity has now become. As I will argue in Chapter 3, over the 1990s, the celebrity turned into such an important commodity that it became a greatly expanded area for content development by the media itself. Today, in a much more highly convergent media environment, where cross-media and cross-platform content and promotion has become the norm, the manufacture of and trade in celebrity has become a commercial strategy for media organisations of all kinds and not just the promotions and publicity sectors. Network and cable television, in particular, has demonstrated its ability to produce celebrity from nothing – without any need to establish the individual's ability, skill, or extraordinariness, as the precondition for public attention. The phenomenon of *Big Brother* made that clear, initially, and the global success of reality TV formats of all kinds has been built upon that foundation.

Usefully, this helps to remind us that celebrity is not only a discursive effect but also a commodity, one that is produced, traded and marketed by the media and publicity industries. In this context, its primary function is commercial and promotional. Indeed, quite early on, Andrew Wernick, in *Promotional Culture*, defined the 'star' solely in such terms: 'A star is anyone whose name and fame has been built up to the point where reference to them, via mention, mediatized representation or live appearance, can serve as a promotional booster in itself' (1991: 106). In such a formulation, the celebrity is defined instrumentally, in terms of the role they play within the operation of the mass media, promotion and publicity industries.

To move towards a definition, then: celebrity is a genre of representation and a discursive effect; it is a commodity traded by the promotions, publicity, and media industries that produce these representations and their effects; and it is a cultural formation that has a social function we can better understand. Increasingly, as we shall see in Chapter 5 and Chapter 6, it is implicated in debates about how identities are constructed in contemporary cultures, and about how the individual self is culturally defined.

PICTURE PERSONALITIES, STARS AND CELEBRITIES

Leo Braudy is one of relatively few to have addressed contemporary celebrity culture by insisting on its continuity with much earlier versions of fame. In *The Frenzy of Renown* (1986), Braudy writes a 'history of fame' that begins in early Roman times and argues that the desire for fame has been a fundamental component of western societies over many centuries. For him, the history of fame provides us with an angle of inspection onto what it means to be an individual, and onto society's shifting definition of achievement, at various points in time (1986: 10). Nevertheless, he acknowledges that modern fame has experienced a degree of inflation as a result of post-Renaissance conceptions of the individual, the collapse of monarchic or religious systems of privilege or distinction in the face of democratisation, and the spread of mass communication. However, these are differences of degree, rather than of substance, in his opinion.

Recently, we have seen an increasing interest in the history of celebrity – typically, in order to extend the temporal horizons of that history. Fred Inglis (2010), and similarly Simon Morgan (2011), locates the beginning of celebrity in the mid-eighteenth century, but insists on what is now a familiar distinction between 'honour and renown' (i.e., fame) and 'glamour and celebrity' (Inglis, 2010: 5). As Inglis sees it, 'the rise of urban democracy, the two-hundred year expansion of its media of communication, together with radical individualization of the modern sensibility made fame a more transitory reward and changed public acclaim from an expression of devotion into one of celebrity' (ibid.: 5). Robert van Krieken takes a slightly different line: while also locating the historical origins of celebrity in the 'court society' of mid-eighteenth century Europe, he argues that an emphasis upon the modernity of celebrity mistakes the 'intensification or acceleration' of the phenomenon 'for its invention' (2012: 11). That is, what is happening now is different in scale and intensity, rather than in kind, to what preceded it. And it is true that there is certainly a growing body of work on celebrity in the late nineteenth century – that is, before the electronic media, but after the development of a mediatised public – which makes a persuasive case for earlier versions of celebrity working in very similar ways to those we witness today (see for example Hindson, 2011).

Nonetheless, and despite also taking the long historical view to contextualise the situation in the twentieth century, Chris Rojek is perhaps speaking for the dominant position when he insists on the fundamental modernity of celebrity: he describes it as 'a phenomenon of mass-circulation newspapers, TV, radio and film' (2001: 16). There are many justifications for such a claim. Some are related to the development of new media technologies. Gamson, for instance, points to the significance of the development of photography as a technology, offering apparently unmediated access to the events represented in the newspaper, while also lending new importance to the representation of the individual. As a consequence of photography's increasing employment in the print media, Gamson argues, the 'dissemination of the face' displaced the dissemination of ideas, laying the ground for the 'publicizing of people' (1994: 21). Further in this vein, Alexander Walker has pointed to the importance of the film close-up, that most individualising of techniques, which offered a new kind of spectacle to the mass audience, exciting new forms of desire (Walker, 1970: 21).

Like Rojek, I am inclined to the standard view – which is that the growth of celebrity is historically linked to the spread of the mass media (particularly the visual media). Increasingly too, as Rojek's *Fame Attack* (2012) argues at length, it is also connected to the invention of public relations and the growth of the promotions and publicity industries from the beginning of the twentieth century.[3] In fact, Schickel argues, the development of these industries made celebrity a necessary invention:

> [D]uring the period – roughly 1895–1920 – when the first blocks of the modern celebrity system were sliding into place everything was improvisatory, primitive. Something more was needed, something that could, on a fairly regular basis, provide the public with a reliable supply of sensations together with an equally steady, glamorous, and easy-to-follow real-life serial adventure. Something that could, as well, allow the press to return to a slightly more passive role in gathering and presenting the news of these creatures, not force it constantly to risk its reputation in prodigies of invention. (Schickel, 1985: 33–4)

Richard Schickel is perhaps most categoric in his uncompromising claim that 'there was no such thing as celebrity prior to the beginning of the twentieth century' (ibid.: 21). Before that, he suggests, we had people who were successful and therefore famous. That changed, he argues, on 24 June 1916, when Mary Pickford signed the first million dollar film contract with Adolph Zukor:

> It was at the moment this deal made headlines that reward began to detach itself from effort and from intrinsic merit, when the old reasonable correlation between what (and how) one did and what one received for doing it became tenuous (and, in the upper reaches of show biz, invisible). (Schickel, 1985: 47)

There are other contenders for the pivotal moment, of course, although most nominate a point in the first two decades of the American motion picture industry, when competition between independent producers was intense and new strategies were being sought to market their products. Film historians like to cite what is usually regarded as the first occasion when publicity is deliberately manipulated in order to build interest in a star. In 1910, producer Carl Laemmle (so the story goes) planted a false story in a St Louis newspaper that reported Florence Lawrence – an actress then known as 'the Biograph Girl' – had been killed in a trolley-car accident. Laemmle immediately denounced the story as a fake and staged a highly public appearance where Lawrence was mobbed by her 'relieved and allegedly adoring public' (Schickel, 1985: 37).

Neal Gabler's biography of newspaper columnist Walter Winchell suggests yet another point of origin and locates it where the representations of the private life of celebrities were first developed, in the modern newspaper:

> In 1925, at a time when the editors of most newspapers were reluctant to publish even something as inoffensive as the notice of an impending birth for fear of crossing the boundaries of good taste, Winchell introduced a revolutionary column that reported who was romancing whom, who was cavorting

with gangsters, who was ill or dying, who was suffering financial difficulties, which spouses were having affairs, which couples were about to divorce, and dozens of other secrets, peccadilloes and imbroglios that had previously been concealed from public view. In doing so, he not only broke a long standing taboo; he suddenly, and singlehandedly expanded the purview of American journalism. (1995: xii)

Gabler's contextualisation of Winchell supports his view that the high profile journalist had 'helped inaugurate a new mass culture of celebrity':

> ... centred only on New York and Hollywood and Washington, fixated on personalities, promulgated by the media, predicated on publicity, dedicated to the ephemeral and grounded on the principle that notoriety confers power. This culture would bind to an increasingly diverse, mobile and atomised nation until *it* became, in many respects, America's dominant ethos, celebrity consciousness our new common denominator. (ibid.: xiii)

Boorstin also located a shift in the content in popular magazines that takes place in the early 1920s. Looking at mass circulation magazines such as *The Saturday Evening Post* and *Collier's*, he noted that 74 per cent of the 'subjects of biographical interest' appearing in their pages in five sample years between 1901 and 1914 came from 'politics, business and the professions'. After 1922, however, 'well over half of them came from the world of entertainment' (1971: 59). Marshall (1997), similarly, tells us that the demand for celebrity material produced a brand new sector of special interest publications during this period. 'Celebrity itself', he says, 'generated an entire industry by the second decade of the twentieth century with the emergence of movie fan magazines (*Moving Picture World*, later followed by *Photoplay, Modern Screen* and *Silver Screen*) that openly celebrated movie stars and their lives' (1997: 8).

Of course, a phenomenon as culturally pervasive as celebrity must have numerous points of origin, numerous points of change. The clearest location at which we might start to chart its various histories, however, seems to be the American motion picture industry at the beginning of the twentieth century. Incorporating the residue of the press agentry networks developed around live theatre and vaudeville, and seeking a means of industrialising the marketing of their new product – the narrative feature film – the nascent American film industry experiences a number of significant shifts that result in the marketing of the 'picture personality' and, later on, 'the star'.

Initially, motion pictures did not include cast lists and actors were not promoted as identities independent of the roles they played on film. The change in these practices around 1910 has been the subject of an extensive historiographic debate.[4] It seems that a number of determinants were in play. Initially, it may have been that the actors themselves were reluctant to advertise their involvement in case it tainted their reputations as dramatic performers in live theatre, or it may have been the studios' fear that promoting individual actors would give them a degree of market power that would ultimately cost the producers money. Or it may simply have been that the studios were unaware that the personalities on display were potentially more powerful drawcards than the narratives to which they contributed their performances. De Cordova traces these issues through his account of the 'picture personalities' (the phrase used at the time) that emerged once the producers began to include a cast list and to credit individual performers. De Cordova's description of its deployment suggests that the phrase is quite accurate in its focus on the production of a performer's personality through the promotional discourses available at the time:

> Personality existed as an effect of the representation of character in a film – or, more accurately, as an effect of the representation of character across a number of films. It functioned primarily to ascribe a unity to the actor's various appearances in films. However, although personality was primarily an effect of the representation of character within films, the illusion that it had its basis outside the film was consistently maintained. (1990: 86)

We can see here the early basis for the privileging of the private self ('the personality') as the object of publicity that is characteristic of contemporary celebrity. Its commercial function in these early days was to build an interest in the individual performer and a desire to see them perform the same personality repeatedly on the screen in new productions. Thus it was important to maintain a tight fit between the personality constructed on the screen and the personality constructed through the promotional discourses:

> ... discourse about the player's existence outside of the films emerged merely as an extension of the existence already laid out within the films. The illusion that was operative was that the player's real personality (as represented in magazines) preceded and caused the representation of personality on the screen. (ibid.: 87–8)

This formation of the picture personality did not last long, however. By 1914, De Cordova argues, a shift had begun to occur in the promotional discourse that would take us from the picture personality – where the personality was a coherent construct promotionally integrated with the screen performances – to the star: 'With the emergence of the star, the question of the player's existence outside his or her work in film became the primary focus of discourse. The private lives of the players were constituted as a site of knowledge and truth' (ibid.: 98). According to other accounts, such as Gamson's, this was a shift that took quite a while to accomplish, and moved through a number of subtle variations. For instance, Gamson notes the strategy used by publicists to tie in a star's image with their current film role well after the period De Cordova nominates. What Gamson describes is the merging of on-screen and off-screen identities as a continual strategic process, with frequent modifications to suit the role being promoted, as the star's identity was made highly responsive to the commercial requirement to promote their current vehicle (Gamson, 1994: 26–7). The shift De Cordova describes may have occurred quite gradually, but its key symptom would become progressively more visible – that is, the disarticulation of the 'true' identity of the star from the aggregated personalities they played on screen.

This carried significant industrial consequences. While the development of the star turned the individual into a commodity to be marketed and traded with greater freedom and flexibility by the industry, it also gave that star access to a new kind of power. They could now construct a relationship with their audience that was independent of the vehicles in which they appeared. With this shift, the individual star had a personal and professional interest in promoting themselves – and not just the latest product in which they had played a role – through the media. Hence we have the constitution of a new source of information for the media and a new means of constructing an identity through the media. Conversely, while the cultural prominence of the stars massively accelerated over the next few years, this created its own problems – even for those who originally stood to profit from this acceleration the most. The studios now had to manage a media presence that had its own personal and professional interests to pursue, while maintaining the commercial value of the star commodity they had helped to create. In some cases – the Fatty Arbuckle scandal, for instance, or the tangled mess of relationships involving Douglas Fairbanks and Mary Pickford – this raised serious issues for the industry's social acceptability.

As the picture personality gave way to the star, a new tier of promotion, publicity and image management entered the media industries. David Marshall (1997) talks about the film star as the apotheosis of the ideologies of individualism he sees embedded in celebrity in general and possibly as the most empowered individual category of celebrity he examines. His discussion of film celebrity emphasises the centrality of freedom, independence and individualism in the discourses used to construct the film star, as well as the commercial significance of the independence of the relationship between the star and their audience. This independence, of course, required management by a third party in most cases – hence the advent of the agent to the business – but this was a third party who was employed by the stars themselves. For successful film stars, celebrity carried a certain amount of power and autonomy as long as it was managed well.

What was crucial here, as Marshall also points out following the lead of Richard Dyer, was the fact that these stars' celebrity had a particular content. In the celebration of their American Dream lifestyles and the media's elaboration of the trappings of their success, Hollywood stars provided a 'wedding of consumer culture with democratic aspirations' (Marshall, 1997: 9). Dyer's work throughout the 1970s and 1980s (1979, 1986), as well as Marshall's own *Celebrity and Power* (1997), is devoted substantially to explaining the comprehensiveness with which western cultures have accepted the film star as a form of public personality with whom they identify, in whom they invest and maintain a personal interest, and to whom is ascribed a value that is cultural or social rather than merely economic.

The development of celebrity in fields other than cinema has its own histories of course and, in some cases, the cultural content they carry is significantly different too. However, and notwithstanding the influence now exerted by the representation of celebrities from a range of industrial locations – sport, popular music, television – in the print media and on television, the development of the film star is perhaps the most elaborate and socially grounded instance of the broad phenomenon of modern celebrity. There are limits to its usefulness as an exemplary case, though. It remains distinctive because of its complex capacity so far to maintain a relationship between the star's celebrity – which mostly insists on their separateness from the person on the screen – and the films in which they have appeared. The film star, even iconic performers such as Clint Eastwood, is continually drawing attention to what they do as a performance and will talk of their careers in terms of a 'body of work'. This is not so much the case with, for instance, the television celebrity. John Langer (1981), many years ago, proposed such a distinction: that film created stars, while television created personalities. Stars develop their reputation by playing someone else. In some cases, these performances retain aspects of a consistently constructed public identity (as with Arnold Schwarzenegger, for instance), while in other cases, the star is known for their ability to submerge their public identity completely in the role being played (as is typical of Robert De Niro, Cate Blanchett, or Johnny Depp). In television, much more categorically, this latter effect is not meant to occur. Personalities simply perform (what the audience sees as) themselves, and the more seamlessly the better (although, as James

Bennett reminds us [2011], this apparent seamlessness is only achieved through the application of a high degree of professionalism and skill). Indeed, one of the key attributes of the television personality is their ability to appear to eliminate the distance between their performance and themselves. They also operate within a different semiotic economy. Stars seem to be able to continually accrue meanings through successive appearances: television personalities, by contrast, are in danger of exhausting the meanings they generate by continually drawing upon them in order to perform at all.

I think Langer's remains a useful distinction (*pace* Bennett, 2011) particularly when we reflect on its parallel with De Cordova's history of the picture personality in early Hollywood – where promotional discourse attempted to construct a close correlation between the performance on screen and the discursive construction of a private self. Television would seem to be replicating that approach in the strategies it uses to promote some of its personalities today, with the marketing of *Survivor* and other reality television formats only the most recent instances of its deployment. That said, it is also true that the distinction between the film star and the television personality looks much less relevant now than it once did: when, for instance, we see how radically the arrival of the reality television celebrity has changed the landscape. As Frances Bonner has argued, the distinctions that Langer proposed have lost some of their pertinence 'as celebrity culture has become so large a part of our mediated culture' in general (2011: 75). Furthermore, television's centrality to celebrity culture has increased – through the rise of the reality TV celebrity, and as it has converged with other media platforms. There is also the criticism that James Bennett makes of Langer's account of the television personality: it implies that television produces 'a form of celebrity that is inferior to other realms' (ibid.:15) or that 'stardom' is simply not possible on television – something directly challenged by Alice Leppert and Julie Wilson's useful (2011) discussion of *The Hills*' Lauren Conrad as the first reality TV 'star'. Bennett's book is aimed, then, at rethinking the specificity of television in the context of the current formations of celebrity culture, and at understanding the different ways in which television celebrity is produced and circulated – something that the rich body of work now being produced on reality TV is also concerned with investigating.

To complete this section, it would be appropriate to talk about the migration of celebrity online to celebrity websites, to blogs, chatrooms and fansites, and to social media such as Twitter. However, I am going to deal with the online celebrity at some length in Chapter 3, and again in Chapter 6, so I will defer that discussion until then.

THE SPREAD OF CELEBRITY CULTURE

As I noted at the beginning of this chapter, it is the pervasiveness of celebrity culture that marks out the contemporary version. Discourses of celebrity invade all kinds of sites today: from contests in shopping malls looking for pre-teen celebrity look-alikes, to the management of major political campaigns. All demonstrate the importance of publicity, promotion and the exploitation of the media event. Boorstin noted that the pseudo event had been part of American politics since the presidency of Franklin D. Roosevelt. Many regarded the election of Ronald Reagan as the point where the production lines of celebrity and politics most emphatically converged in the USA, but the election of Barack Obama is an even more dramatic case. In the UK, accounts of the prominence of 'spin' – the tireless management of the media's access to and deployment of information – in preparing the way for the election of Tony Blair's 'New Labour', became the accepted explanation for the comprehensiveness of the Tories' defeats in successive elections. Indeed, when Blair began to experience a backlash at a number of public events during 2002, in what was the precursor to the collapse of his electoral support, this was widely regarded as a response to the perceived influence of public relations 'spin doctors' driving principles out of politics altogether.

In business, Rakesh Khurana (2003) has chronicled what he describes as the 'irrational quest for charismatic CEOs': the 1980s break with the traditions of managerial capitalism that resulted in swashbuckling CEOs leading the businesses of the 1990s – and this has continued into the present. Where once, some can still remember, the individuality of the professional manager had been subordinated in exchange for the security of their place in the corporate hierarchy, the more volatile industrial environment of the 'new economy' increasingly sought its salvation in 'charismatic authority' (what Khurana describes as 'celebrity CEOs' [2003: 168–72]). The development of celebrity became a commercial asset in the business world, just as it was in the entertainment industries, and in figures such as Donald Trump and Alan Sugar, the two sectors merged through the alchemy of reality television (both became stars of the reality TV game-doc *The Apprentice* in, respectively, the US and UK versions). It is now relatively common for the CEOs of major companies to appear on television hawking their company's products, on magazine covers and in newspaper features promoting themselves, and to employ ghost writers to produce self-serving autobiographies. Within their own industry, in particular, celebrity fed upon itself. As Khurana describes it, in the labour market for CEOs in America at the time, 'stories, gossip, and legends' about the 'charismatic' executive simply travelled farther than those about others, 'irrespective of various individuals' abilities or accomplishments' (ibid.: 152). Even from within the slightly 'alternative' and nerdy world of computer companies, figures such as Bill Gates and the late Steve Jobs emerged to become household names.

In 1991 Andrew Wernick published a highly critical diagnosis of contemporary western culture that claimed it was dominated by the processes of publicity and promotion. Originating in a critique of the pervasiveness of the practice of advertising and its underlying ideologies, Wernick's book accused contemporary commercial popular culture of a generic 'bad faith'. For him, the influence of advertising and its commercial logics had resulted in the phoney, the constructed and the simulated taking over the cultural landscape.[5] John Hartley, coming from a very different angle in that his view of contemporary popular culture vigorously rejects the elite critique of the popular, also acknowledged the pervasive influence of promotional discourse within contemporary popular culture. He went so far as to coin a term, 'the smiling professions', for the range of occupations, functions and personnel employed in the broad fields of the media, publicity and promotion (1992: Chapter 5). However, unlike Wernick, Hartley argued that, far from publicity being an enemy of 'the public', it was through publicity that 'the public' actually came into being. Publicity, for Hartley, became one of the fundamental enabling components in the construction of contemporary public culture, and 'the smiling professions' its primary functionaries:

> [T]here is a new development in the history of looking: the public has slipped, perhaps decisively, from the disciplinary grasp of educational and governmental authorities into the gentler hands of the smiling professions. Smiling has become one of the most important public virtues of our times, a uniform that must be worn on the lips of those whose social function it is to create, sustain, tutor, represent and make images of the public – to call it into discursive being. (1992: 121–2)

As a result, 'in a market where years of experience can be outbid by a squirt of hairspray, it is not learning but looks, not the cerebral but celebrity, that mark the winners' (Hartley, 1996: 36). Hartley is not as offended by this as Wernick – rather his project was to achieve an accurate recognition of this situation by journalism educators, so that they might better understand how to educate their students to deal with it.

Hartley's argument usefully reminds us that the spread of celebrity is not just the consequence of an accumulation of publicity handouts, advertisements, chat show interviews, or the shock-horror revelations in the tabloid screamers. The really interesting (and perhaps most surprising) aspect of celebrity is the degree to which it has become integrated into the cultural processes of our daily lives. As Richard Dyer points out, a 'star's image is also what people say or write about him or her, the way the image is used in other contexts such as advertisements, novels, pop songs, and finally the way the star can become part of the coinage of everyday speech' (1986: 2–3). The celebrity has a generally cultural pervasiveness, as the cultural meanings of and associations with the star leak into all kinds of locations in our daily lives – expanding the range of territories into which the media industries and their 'smiling professionals' now gain (or control) access.

Leo Braudy puts a positive spin on this new exorbitance of celebrity – responding to the human 'urge to be unique' – as he too stresses the contemporary expansion of the possibilities for fame. That fame has been disconnected from achievement seems not to worry him too much either: 'the dream of fame', he says, has always been 'inseparable from the idea of personal freedom'. And so, in a perverse way, the more available fame is, and the less 'deserved' it is, the more it operates as a means of providing a 'personal justification' for the individual's existence (1986: 7). The tight ideological connection between the discourses of celebrity and democracy and their integration into the legitimation of market capitalism that Marshall's work describes, then, is reprocessed by Braudy's account into a productive and consoling feature of contemporary society.

Tempting though these big connections are, they tend to obscure the fact that what constitutes celebrity in one cultural domain may be quite different in another. I have already discussed the specificity of the film star's celebrity, in comparison with that of the television personality. Dyer's work on film stars reflects this, dealing with the particular meanings of individual stars rather than simply citing them as instances of a broadly enacted process of cultural production (1979, 1986). Marshall's 1997 study also, while in some respects not entirely in sympathy with Dyer's, reinforces the importance of distinguishing between different kinds of celebrity in terms of the media through which they are predominantly reproduced and in terms of the industry from which they have emerged. Consequently, while this larger over-determining process is the primary subject of this book, we should not lose sight of the crucial distinctions that remain active within it.

Joe Moran's work on literary celebrity is a good example of how such distinctions might be made. Moran acknowledges that the literary celebrity is indeed subject to the same systemic structures as any other kind, competing for space in the newspapers, television chat shows and so on. He also argues that literary publishing operates 'an elaborate system of representations in its own right, produced and circulated across a wide variety of media' (2000: 3–4). Through case studies of the works and reputations of John Updike, Philip Roth and Kathy Acker, Moran argues that the literary texts themselves play a part in this system of celebrity production because of the way they address, mediate and complement already existing meanings. The literary celebrity is at least partly produced by their own writing, as it intersects with other discourses produced through other textual forms. An author such as Salman Rushdie, for instance, is going to be read through a complex set of intertextual references, to which each successive book makes its own particular contribution. As a result, Moran insists, literary celebrity, 'works as much through the sphere of textual representation [in the actual literary text] as it does through the material processes of cultural production and consumption' (ibid.: 3).

From one point of view, this may not be significantly different from the processes through which the film star's meanings are accrued. The star's 'work', too, has that inevitably self-referential potential as each successive performance contributes to the story of their career (although they are not usually in the same sense the 'authors' of their own work). Moran's insistence probably reflects the fact that literary fans might like to think of themselves as pursuing an interest in an artist rather than a celebrity, in order to locate themselves on a slightly higher plane of cultural consumption. This is despite the fact that literary festivals, writers' festivals and the like attract mass audiences who behave much like any other kind of fan. They want to see their favourite author in the flesh in order to gain an insight into what they are 'really like' – and maybe buy a t-shirt or get their book autographed. Like other kinds of celebrity, the literary figure will create their prominence through publicity campaigns, interviews on talk shows, in-store book-signings, personal appearances, feature articles in newspapers, press coverage of their private lives, entries in gossip columns, biographies, advertisements, and promotional gimmicks, as well as that whole other dimension of publicity that comes with their being taken up as serious writers within schools and universities.

One area where it is essential to acknowledge some differentiation is sport. The sports star celebrity is a particularly interesting case because, as David Giles (among others) points out, sport is 'one of the few areas of public life that is truly meritocratic': sports stars 'can *prove* they are the best' (2000: 107). Therefore, their cultural prominence can be regarded as deserved. Further, sports stars perform, unequivocally, as themselves. Andrews and Jackson (2001) suggest that where performers in film or television adopt 'fictive identities' to do what they do, sport offers the spectacle of '*real* individuals participating in unpredictable contests'. This creates a veneer of authenticity, they argue, which sets the sports star apart from 'other, more explicitly manufactured, cultural realms' (presumably, such as film or television). The downside here, they also suggest, is that the sports star is therefore especially vulnerable to a drop in their performance, which can result in a rapid decline in the public's interest in them and thus in their commercial and professional potential (2001: 8). Finally, Gary Whannell (2002) argues, the sports star is especially articulated to discourses of achievement, excellence, and transcendence – often explicitly tied up with definitions of nationality and ethnicity. The quality of what they do matters a great deal, not only to the industry but also, in many instances, to the nation (just ask Michael Phelps, Kevin Pietersen, or David Beckham about that).

On the face of it, the fact that discourses of excellence are so thoroughly embedded within sports would suggest that the sports celebrity does not easily fit the general pattern we are describing. However, while the process through which they come to public attention may be different from that which affects celebrities from other domains, sports stars are certainly subject to the same mass-mediated processes of celebritisation we have been examining. It would be fair to say that the public interest in many high profile sports stars is focused primarily on their private lives, rather than on their sporting achievements. Indeed, there are many examples – David Beckham would be one, Tiger Woods another – where despite a decline in their sporting achievements, sports celebrities are still capable of drawing a crowd, selling a newspaper, attracting hits on a website, or followers on Twitter.

It may be that once we move beyond the processes of production, the differences between the different locations of celebrity do not matter that much. The celebrity may have achieved things that suggest they 'deserve' their eminence, but these are not going to protect that individual from the celebrity process, nor affect how it actually operates over time. Once that process kicks in it has its own logic that, say, Real Madrid's Cristiano Ronaldo must accept while he goes about his business as a footballer. The effects of celebrity simply contribute to the cultural context within which he must ply his trade. David Marshall introduces another dimension to this, however. He organises *Celebrity and Power* (1997) around the assumption that different industries will not only produce their celebrities in different ways, but also that their celebrities will generate different kinds of meanings. He provides accounts of celebrity as it works in cinema, television and the music industry. Through case studies of Tom Cruise, Oprah Winfrey and New Kids on the Block, he compares and contrasts the various organisational systems and regimes of publicity and promotion. He also argues that there are distinct semiotic and discursive regimes built up around the different industrial sites for celebrity. Not only are their celebrities produced through different systems but the meanings they generate also privilege different groups of discourses. According to Marshall's study, the film star is structured through the discourses of individualism, the television personality constructs their celebrity through 'conceptions of familiarity', and the music star articulates their meanings to discourses of 'authenticity'. Marshall helps us to see the particular meanings and distinctions that are important and valued within that particular media culture and within that community of fans or consumers.

Finally, here, we need to recognise that the development of the internet has dramatically affected the public's capacity to directly participate in, if not control, the processes we have described. Users of the many celebrity gossip sites comment and criticise, remediating content and feeding stories into mainstream news media. In many cases, the comments posted on these sites have minimal legal, regulatory, or even commercial constraints upon them to limit what is said. As we shall see in Chapter 3, while the internet has a major effect on how the mass media celebrities operate and how their personae are collaboratively constructed, it has also created a new domain of 'micro-celebrity' (Senft, 2008) where ordinary people create a web presence and a public persona through blogs and social media such as Twitter. It is true that much of the celebrity constructed within these social networks, and indeed the patterns of micro-celebrity itself, tend to be limited to these networks; however, they do work in ways that mimic larger systems and can from time to time mutate into mainstream celebrity. Nevertheless, celebrity takes on new functions and meanings in these contexts as it is effectively turned into a demotic strategy of identity formation for the people 'formerly known as the audience' (Rosen, 2006).

TAXONOMIES OF FAME

The approach I am developing in this book deals with celebrity as a media process that is coordinated by an industry, and as a commodity or text which is productively consumed by audiences and fans. I don't pretend that this is the only way we can approach the phenomenon. There have been many attempts to deal with celebrity through the analysis of a set of properties associated with the individuals concerned. As a result, there are taxonomies of celebrity – systems that categorise the celebrity in terms of the meanings they generate, or the power they possess, or the political and social determinants responsible for their public profile, and so on. One of the earliest taxonomies is Alberoni's, which distinguishes two kinds of social-political elites. The first is composed of people who possess 'political, economic or religious power', whose decisions 'have an influence on the present and future fortunes of the society which they direct'. The second group is what we now think of as celebrities and they are people 'whose institutional power is very limited or non-existent, but whose doings and way of life arouse a considerable and sometimes even a maximum degree of interest' (Alberoni, 1972: 72). Since these individuals do not exercise any institutional influence over the 'lives and future expectations of members of the society', Alberoni describes them as a 'powerless elite'. Marshall (1997) has demonstrated why this underestimates the cultural power possessed by the celebrity, and his argument is also reprised in Turner et al. (2000). Neal Gabler, though, posits an alternative view in his history of Walter Winchell and the American media in the 1920s and 30s, when he says that 'power was really a function not of wealth or breeding or talent or connections but of publicity'. Fame, according to Gabler, actually came to constitute power itself, as 'social authority in the early thirties had been turned on its head: it now derived from the media' (1995: 184–5). There is another dimension to this that Alberoni also misunderstands and therefore discounts. This is precisely what has made celebrity so interesting to us in recent years: its increasing purchase on our experience of everyday life and its implication in the construction and definitions of cultural identity. Taxonomies, in general, share this failing in that they tend to underestimate the importance of the interests of those who consume celebrity, focusing instead on elaborating the character of the celebrity itself.

James Monaco (1978) sets up three categories of celebrity. The 'hero' is someone who has actually done something spectacular to attract attention in the first place: astronauts, for instance, would fall into this category. The 'star' is the second category and they, according to Monaco, achieve prominence through the development of a public persona that is more important than their professional profile. Crudely, the movie actor is only a star if they become more interesting than their roles. Monaco suggests that many politicians aspire towards becoming a 'star' as a means of advancing their political careers. The third category is the 'quasar', and this roughly corresponds to what Turner et al. (2000) have referred to as the 'accidental celebrity'. This is the person who has become the focus of attention initially through no fault of their own, and through a process over which they can have very little control. Monica Lewinsky, London bombing survivor John Tulloch, kidnap victim Joanne Lees, or Australian disaster survivor Stuart Diver would be examples of this category.[6] The 'quasar', though, might be better understood as an effect of the contemporary operation of the news media rather than a category of celebrity. Any examination of how it worked as a cultural phenomenon would need to concentrate on the industrial conditions that assisted its production.[7]

Chris Rojek (2001: Chapter 1) has developed the most interesting set of categories, in my view, and the one which has been most widely adopted in recent years. Initially, his system does tend to repeat the kinds of distinctions we have already met; it outlines three broad types of celebrity, which are categorised in terms of how celebrity is earned or attributed. According to Rojek's model, celebrity is 'ascribed' through blood relations (the British royal family, say), 'achieved' in open competition (sports stars), or 'attributed' by the media (television personalities). To some extent, the model implies a hierarchical progression so that 'attribution' follows as a consequence of achievement. As we have seen, however, the attribution of celebrity can occur without any significant achievement as its precondition and this is increasingly frequent within the media today.

Unlike the authors of most of the other taxonomies, however, Rojek acknowledges the limitations of this three-part model in its application to contemporary celebrity. In particular, he sees the need to address the heightened intensity and the apparent arbitrariness of the modern media's concentration on the celebrity and he has done this by coining the term 'celetoid'. The celetoid enjoys a hyper-visibility but also an especially short and unpredictable lifespan: the category includes film stars and television personalities as well as the kinds of figures we have been describing as 'accidental' celebrities or 'quasars'. (There is also a sub-category, the 'celeactor': this is the fictional character like Ali G or Dame Edna Everage who behaves in the public eye as if they were a 'real' celebrity.) Crucial factors are the sharpness of the trajectory their public careers typically describe (the celetoid may go from high visibility to virtual invisibility in a matter of weeks in some instances), and the way interest is manufactured around them as a means of promoting particular media products such as newspapers. What Rojek describes, then, is actually the logic and rhythm of the media production around such figures, rather than the attributes of particular people.

What is particularly distinctive about Rojek's approach is that he devotes a chapter to seriously addressing the other side of celebrity – the transgressive, notorious, or criminal figure (such as the Unabomber, for instance). Rojek accepts that celebrity in general is largely confirmatory of dominant values and that the notoriety he examines is definitively transgressive. Nonetheless, he defends the widening of his focus as a means of recognising the public impact of such figures: their capacity to generate fans, followers and copycat performances, for instance, as well as their effect on the 'public consciousness'. (He uses the equation, 'celebrity = public consciousness', as a means of explaining why he includes the 'notorious' as an aspect of celebrity within the study [2001: 8]). It's a fair point and it does seem worthwhile to consider how someone such as a convicted serial killer might generate fans – because they clearly do. However, the pro-social, pro-individualist and pro-capitalist discourses that construct the more conventional versions of celebrity are sufficiently consistent to suggest we might need another term to organise our discussion of the specificity of the cultural impact of the notorious or criminal figure, even though many aspects of this impact reflect the workings of celebrity. Consequently, while there are some essays which have focused on this kind of celebrity (e.g., Schmid, 2006), it remains an undeveloped part of the field of celebrity studies.

THE SOCIAL FUNCTIONS OF CELEBRITY

I began this chapter by looking at Boorstin's critique of celebrity as a means of acknowledging those accounts that regard celebrity as the epitome of all that is trivial, superficial, meretricious and deplorable about contemporary popular culture. There are certainly plenty of these, particularly in the opinion columns of newspapers and magazines – precisely the media, of course, where the discourses of celebrity circulate most vigorously. Some of these complaints have familiar origins in the elite critique of popular culture and probably have little new to say about celebrity in particular. Others, however, focus upon celebrity in detail so as to describe the function it performs for society and to explain why that is bad. Representative would be a view of our culture's interest in celebrity that regarded it as a form of mass delusion, what Schickel calls 'the illusion of intimacy' (1985: 4). This view implies contempt for the experience of the popular audience and offers no possibility of a positive or productive social function for the celebrity.

Such arguments are usually enclosed within long-running critical debates about cultural populism, tabloidisation and a diagnosis of the condition of the democratic public sphere – themes that will be discussed later on in this book. At this stage, however, I would like to review explanations of the more productive social and cultural functions that celebrity and its culture seems likely to perform for us today. The fact that celebrity has extended its purchase upon the public imagination across cultures and over time provides at least *prima facie* evidence that it might be performing some kind of social function for its consumers.

The first set of explanations of the productive social function of celebrity has already been referred to briefly earlier on. This is the argument that the celebrity generates para-social interactions that operate as a means of compensating for changes in the social construction of the communities within which many of us live. At one time the term 'para-social' may have described an impoverished surrogate for 'real' social relations, but that implication tends not to mark the most recent accounts.[8] The most obvious examples of para-social relationships dealt with in the contemporary literature are the popular reactions to the deaths of high profile celebrities – Elvis Presley (Marcus, 1991), John Lennon (Elliott, 1999), and most dramatically, Princess Diana (Re:Public, 1997). These are instances where large numbers of people around the world respond to what they think of as 'real' emotional attachments with figures they know only through their representations in the media. It has taken some time even for those working in celebrity studies to realise that we need to take the testimony of such people at face value as the first step to better understanding this phenomenon. Indeed, some of the most resonant contributions to the literature have accepted and reflected upon their own investment in the para-social interaction with, for instance, Princess Diana and put cultural theory to work as a means of understanding it. (Richard Johnson's highly personal essay in 1999, for instance, is an example of this and is discussed in Chapter 5.) Also, as we shall see in Chapter 3, celebrities' take-up of social media has challenged some of the assumptions which had hitherto framed the description of the fan's relation to the celebrity as para-social: the capacity to communicate directly online doesn't easily fit that description (Marwick and boyd, 2011).

A second group of explanations gather around the celebrity's role as a location for the interrogation and elaboration of cultural identity. There are a number of dimensions to this. First, we have the discussion of celebrity as a source of gossip, which is itself understood as an important social process through which relationships, identity, and social and cultural norms are debated, evaluated, modified and shared (Hermes, 1995; Turner et al., 2000). Its expansion as a form of media content has inserted the celebrity into processes of social and personal identity formation that are clearly fundamental. This may have come at the cost of what we might think of as 'real' content – gossip about friends or people we know from direct personal encounters, for instance. However, there seems no intrinsic reason why the partial substitution of a category of content should have negative effects, or change the nature or productivity of the social and communicative processes into which it has been inserted. The second dimension sees the celebrity as a key location for the elaboration of the definition of the individual. Most accounts of the history of celebrity relate it to, among other things, the pairing of the growth of individualism with the rise of democracy.[9] As a result, it is suggested, celebrity operates 'at the very centre of the culture as it resonates with conceptions of individuality that are the ideological ground of Western culture' (Marshall, 1997; x). Marshall describes celebrity as one of the fundamental mechanisms for constructing and maintaining the discursive linkages between consumer capitalism, democracy and individualism. If Marshall is right, then celebrity has a crucial ideological function.

Richard Dyer's *Stars* (1979) was groundbreaking in its proposition that stars worked like 'signs': as semiotic systems embedded with cultural meanings to be actively read and interpreted by their audiences. Dyer argued that we read stars as texts and these texts are both ideologically saturated and discursively constructed. The meanings they generated were the product of a 'structured polysemy': this refers to the 'finite multiplicity of meanings and affects they embody as well as to the attempt to so structure them that some meanings are foregrounded and others are masked or displaced' (1979: 3). The celebrity is not only a semiotic regime, but also the visible tip of a highly contingent field of power relations. Dyer was particularly interested, though, in how society used stars as a means of thinking about the individual: 'they articulate the promise and the difficulty that the notion of the individual presents for all of us who live by it' (1986: 8). The contradictoriness of this process of 'articulation' has been widely acknowledged: while stars might represent 'individualised social types', they do so by actively reconciling competing principles – 'personal identity with social identity, and individualism with conformity' (Chaney, 1993: 145).

Marshall's work extends Dyer's analysis to apply it to celebrities across a range of media and he explains clearly how this process – the construction of the individual and the negotiation of social and cultural identities – works in practice:

> The types of messages that the celebrity provides for the audience are modalised around forms of individual identification, social difference and distinction, and the universality of personality types. Celebrities represent subject positions that audiences can adopt or adapt in their formation of social identities. Each celebrity represents a complex form of audience-subjectivity that, when placed within a system of celebrities, provides the ground in which distinctions, differences, and oppositions are played out. The celebrity, then, is an embodiment of a discursive battleground on the norms of individuality and personality within a culture. (1997: 65)

The reference to normativity, of course, implies a highly specific, sociologically classical, function for the celebrity. Marshall has put a slightly different spin on this, however, through his proposition that the celebrity-commodity provides a very powerful form of legitimation for capitalism's models of exchange and value by demonstrating that the individual has a commercial as well as a cultural value. A range of useful research dealing with reality TV, particularly the most recent work which has focused on the role of class in certain reality formats (Wood and Skeggs, 2011), has developed this dimension considerably, and is making a major contribution to our understandings of the contemporary political and cultural function of the media (Andrejevic, 2004; Hay and Ouellette, 2008; Skeggs and Wood, 2012).

There have been other, less explicitly political, attempts to describe what Rojek calls the 'integrating function' performed by celebrity. To return to an issue noted earlier, the most interesting explores the parallels with religion.[10] Most of these argue that while celebrity culture is not a direct substitute for religion within contemporary society, there is a relationship between them. Some aspects of organised religion have been taken over by the forms of commodification developed in celebrity culture and this is certainly visible in even the briefest examination of television evangelism. Both Giles and Rojek claim that the gap left by the decline in the cultural purchase of organised religion has at least partly been filled by celebrity. As a result, as Rojek puts it, 'post-God celebrity is now one of the mainstays of organising recognition and belonging in a secular society' (2001: 58). At the end of his useful chapter on celebrity and religion, Rojek concludes:

> To the extent that organised religion has declined in the West, celebrity culture has emerged as one of the replacement strategies that promotes new orders of meaning and solidarity. As such, notwithstanding the role that some celebrities have played in destabilising order, celebrity culture is a significant institution in the normative achievement of social integration. (2001: 99)

These accounts of the social function of celebrity reveal new angles of inspection onto the way our culture now generates meaning, significance, pleasure and desire, and in addition to this they offer us some new ways of explaining the distribution and operation of cultural power through the media and the publicity and promotion industries.

CELEBRITY AND THE PUBLICITY INDUSTRIES

Celebrity is an industry that creates highly visible products that most of us buy at one time or another and which play a significant part in our everyday lives. It is also an industry that spends a great deal of its time masking the fact that it exists at all. The point of publicity and promotion is to 'turn advertising into news' (Turner et al., 2000: 31) – to provide free editorial coverage of an event, person, or cause. Good publicists are invisible and good promotional strategies wind up on the front pages of newspapers, not in the gossip or entertainment columns. This can be achieved in many different ways but they must not puncture the illusion upon which the whole game depends: that 'the news' is the product of independent journalism.

We have reached the point where we are beginning to think more about how such a process does actually work. What are the industrial structures required, and upon what relationships – discursive, economic, political, and cultural – do they depend? To argue that celebrity has a social function, that its products are open to semiotic analysis and that it participates directly in the negotiation of cultural identity, is not to deny that the celebrity is also a manufactured commodity, that its development is commercially strategic, and that its trade is one of the fundamental transactions within the cultural and media industries today. The following chapter, then, will focus on the industry that develops and markets the celebrity-as-commodity.

NOTES

1 Gitlin's *Media Unlimited* (2001), the source of our epigraph, is but one example of such a view, and Schickel's *Intimate Strangers* (1985) another, but there are many more.

2 Ian Connell (1992) argued that this less generous motivation was fundamental to celebrity media, and explained such phenomena as the malicious and clearly false stories about celebrities that circulate in the British tabloid press. Andrew Ross (1989), to extend it a little further, stated that the point of much popular culture was to signify its disrespect for the bourgeois values that sought to contain and control it; it is a point repeatedly made in John Hartley's work, and it is a key area of interest for Skeggs and Wood's (2012) interest in the working-class audiences for reality TV.

3 The first independent publicity firm was established in the USA in 1900 (Gamson, 1994: 22).

4 See the articles from Staiger and De Cordova in Gledhill (1991), as well as the accounts presented in Schickel (1985) and De Cordova's later book (1990).

5 While this is in some ways similar to the position taken by Boorstin back in 1961, Wernick's book owes more to the Marxian critiques of the Frankfurt School.

6 Monica Lewinsky needs no explanation, academic John Tulloch's photograph became an iconic referent for the London bombing of 2007, Joanne Lees was tied up and blindfolded by an unknown assailant in the middle of the Australian outback who is believed to have killed her boyfriend, Peter Falconio. A major media story in Australia and the UK in 2001, a number of the British tabloids raised the possibility that she herself was the killer and her story was a fabrication. Stuart Diver was the only survivor of a landslide in the snowfields in Australia in 1999; buried alive for several days in freezing conditions, his survival was seen as miraculous. He avoided publicity about his ordeal, but eventually hired a manager to gain control over the media's interest in his story.

7 There are lots of other taxonomies, of course. A further example would be David Giles's, which is similar in structure to Monaco's except for his division of the first category into two (2000: 115).

8 Joli Jenson (1992) reviews the earlier use of the term, tracing it back to the mid-1950s, and Chris Rojek (2001) provides a good example of the less judgemental contemporary use of the term.

9 Among the writers I deal with in this chapter who make this connection are Monaco (1978), Rojek (2001), Giles (2000), Marshall (1997), and Dyer (1979).

10 Rojek (2001 and 2012).

Part two

Production

2 The Economy of Celebrity

A celebrity is a person whose name has attention-getting, interest-rivetting, and profit-generating value. (Rein, Kotler and Stoller, 1997: 15)

GLOBALISATION AND MEDIA CONVERGENCE

The broad context for this chapter is dominated, overwhelmingly, by two forces: what is customarily described as the globalisation of the media and entertainment industries, and convergence between the technologies used as systems of delivery within the information, entertainment and media indus-tries. While I am not going to go into these two forces in depth here, I need to outline the kinds of importance they have for our understanding of the production of the contemporary celebrity.

The process of globalisation has been subject to some misleading hyperbole in recent years, and therefore it is probably necessary to say, as a reality check, that it is neither as unstoppable nor as universal a force as many pundits would suggest. In fact, once we enquire into the claims made for it, we find that globalisation is not really 'global' at all. In terms of its reach and effects, it is most significant in linking western cultures in the global North and in distributing particular forms of modernisation into Asia (Pertierra and Turner, 2013). Further, and as Toby Miller puts it in *Global Hollywood*, glo-balisation is a 'maddeningly euphemistic term laden with desire, fantasy, fear, attraction – and intellectual imprecision about what it is supposed to describe' (Miller et al., 2001: 18). Boosting the globalisation myth has been politically useful to economic neo-liberals in both conservative and reformist western democratic governments, and so its character and purchase have often been misrepresented for political reasons. Therefore, it is worth reminding our-selves that some kind of economic globalisation is not a particularly novel development: processes of globalisation have been in train for many centu-ries, although they may have passed under a different name – mercantilism, for instance, or colonialism, or imperialism. More specifically, we should remember that certain media industries, such as feature film or popular music production, have long been dominated by transnational corporations and have thus operated 'globally' for decades.

Nevertheless, it is certainly true that the media and entertainment industries constitute a prime site for an examination of the impact of contemporary forms of globalisation where they have become significant, because these industries (and especially television) have been leading the way. Not only have they led globalising processes, but they have also collaborated enthusiastically in the deregulation, privatisation and commercialisation of national or regional media systems, as national broadcasters and media organisations are swallowed up by transnational commercial conglomerates. Consequently, the global media and entertainment system has for some time now been dominated by 'three or four dozen large transnational corporations, with fewer than ten mostly US-based media conglomerates towering over the global market' (Herman and McChesney, 1997: 1). More recently, this number has been reduced to what Hesmondhalgh (following Castells) calls the 'magnificent seven': Vivendi, Disney, Comcast, News Corporation, Time Warner, Sony and Bertelsmann (2013: 195).[1] These organisations spread their costs and maximise their profits by developing products in one location, typically the United States, before selling them across a range of global markets. At their most successful, these products do become truly global commodities: while it is no longer quite so globally dominant as it once was, Hollywood cinema, for instance, remains the international currency of commercial cinema in western countries (see Miller et al., 2001) and a key means of the commodification and marketing of Western culture elsewhere – and this carries consequences for the international visibility of its directors, designers, producers and stars.

The spread and purchase of these transnational companies' interests are extraordinary. Among the holdings of Rupert Murdoch's News Corporation are cable, satellite and terrestrial television interests in Europe, Canada, the USA, Asia and the UK; he has newspaper and magazine interests in Australia, the UK and the USA; and he owns the Twentieth Century Fox film and video production centre – an international publishing conglomerate – as well as the television rights to such major sports as Premier League football (UK) and the National Football League (USA). Despite selling its Time Life book publishing network, Warner Music, and AOL in recent years, Time Warner still has interests in magazine publishing, Warner Bros. film studios, and cable television channels such as HBO, as well as a number of theme parks and retail ventures.

The power of these transnational companies has been built on their pattern of diversifying from their base in one media form across many media platforms. The (short-lived) merger between America On Line (AOL) and Time Warner some years ago perfectly demonstrated this strategy, as it brought together commercial interests in internet service provision, print media, and television and film production. The history of News Corporation tells a similar story. Rupert Murdoch started out in newspaper publishing in a provincial Australian city, moving on to an Australian national daily and a number of metropolitan television channels before purchasing the Fox television network in the USA, and major newspapers in the USA and UK. This pattern of expansion and diversification across media forms and national boundaries has become an industrially entrenched strategy as a result of the 1990s shift towards technological and industrial convergence both in the production industries and in the regulatory environments within which they operated.

It goes without saying that the convergence between systems of delivery in the media, entertainment and information industries has enabled this process to proceed at a hectic pace over the last decade. It is important to recognise, though, its difference from the more longstanding practice of simply spinning off media tie-ins from original content. The traditional model, for instance, is the kind of thing we would see in, say, the promotion of a major film such as *Lord of the Rings: The Two Towers*. The promotion of that film included a new edition of the book upon which the film is based, a DVD/CD and video on sale after the theatrical run had concluded, a computer game, a television documentary on the 'making of' the film, and a whole range of merchandising licences for action figures and so on. What happens as a result of convergence is slightly different, in that it effectively involves the *same* content being delivered by way of different media platforms.

These are the more radical possibilities for what Simone Murray (2003) calls 'content streaming' – the repurposing of content for new media platforms. The traditional distinctions between the content and technologies of, say, broadcasting and subscription mass media, telecommunications, recorded music, and computing, have dissolved. So, for instance, you can play your choice of music on your computer, your phone, your tablet or iPad, your TV, your gaming console, your iPod, or your CD and DVD player – and you can store it virtually so that you never actually possess that musical item as a physical object. This means that there is every commercial reason why those who own the content would make it available over as many media platforms as possible. And if the corporation in question also has a financial interest in providing content to these other platforms, then there is even more reason to take advantage of this convergence of technologies and systems of delivery and the very few additional costs involved. Again, it is worthwhile to remember that historically these industries have been particularly alert to the benefits of such synergies. For many decades, transnational companies in the film, television and popular music industries, in particular, have vigorously pursued vertical integration – that is, corporate control of the full range of industrial processes, from the production of content, software and hardware, to marketing, distribution, exhibition, and delivery to consumers. To expand into new media formats in order to market products originally developed for another media format has made perfect sense for these companies.

The celebrity, of course, is a very useful (perhaps the best!) way of connecting these cross media processes. They become a vehicle for transferring product from one format to the next, a fundamental part of the process of content streaming. In one sense this is not new. The star of a new movie release will routinely do a round of television talk shows to promote the product. What does seem new, however, is the importance of the celebrity as a *branding* mechanism for media products that has assisted their fluent translation across media formats and systems of delivery. As Naomi Klein suggested, celebrity's importance as a means of cross-promotion of this kind is one of the reasons for the increased prominence of sports stars. A high-profile sports star like Michael Jordan or David Beckham can become a 'one-man superbrand' (Klein, 2001: 57), able to move his audiences into new regimes of consumption. This is by no means confined to sports stars, of course. Since 1999, *Forbes* magazine has been publishing its 'Celebrity 100', a ranking of celebrities based not just on their earnings but also on a calculation of the 'power' they have as a brand. (The top three for 2012 were Jennifer Lopez, Oprah Winfrey, and Justin Bieber.)

The conditions I have been describing are more enabling than determining perhaps, but they have had a profound impact on the cultural and economic power of the celebrity in general. The celebrity's usefulness to the cross-media expansion of the major media and entertainment industry conglomerates has translated into an enhanced value for the celebrity as a commodity. It is to this category, the celebrity-commodity, I want to turn next.

THE CELEBRITY-COMMODITY

Celebrities are developed to make money. Their names and images are used to market lingerie, swimwear, fragrances, and sports shoes, as well as the products of the entertainment industries: films, DVDs, magazines, newspapers, television programmes – even the evening news. Media entrepreneurs want celebrities involved with their projects because they believe this will help them attract audiences. Film producers use stars as a means of attracting investment to their projects, marketers use celebrity endorsements as a means of profiling and branding their products, television programmes feature guest appearances from celebrities to build their audiences, and sports promoters use celebrity athletes to attract media attention and increase the size of the gate. Celebrity also makes money for the individual concerned, of course and it does this in two ways. While they are cultural workers and are paid for their labour, celebrities are also 'property' (Dyer, 1986: 5): that is, they are a financial asset to those who stand to gain from their commercialisation – networks, music production companies, agents, managers, and finally the celebrities themselves. The celebrity can develop their public persona as a commercial asset and their career choices, in principle, should be devoted to focusing on that objective. As the asset appreciates – as the celebrity's fame spreads – so does its earning capacity.

The development of the celebrity's public profile, then, is a serious business and, as we saw earlier, it is usually placed in the hands of a third party – most often a manager (although in some markets the division of labour may vary so that theatrical agents or network publicists take on this role). Ideally, this third party will have a long-term interest in the celebrity's commercial success. After all, their own income is linked to their effective management (and protection) of the celebrity's personal and commercial interests. In practice, however, it may not always be that simple. Occasionally, the agent or manager may find that they have a compelling but short-term interest in maximising the current returns from their celebrity-commodity: when the celebrity becomes a particularly 'hot' property, for instance, for a limited period of time. Further, certain sections of the sports and entertainment industries do not normally offer strong prospects of longevity (popular music would be one, and sport another), and so anyone handling a celebrity in such a field has to make a judgement about their long-term prospects before deciding what kind of strategy to pursue. In general, the third party – whether a manager, agent, or network publicist – will have a number of celebrities on their books. This not only varies and spreads their investment, and thus their commercial risk, but it also reflects their particular need to protect themselves against the fact that they do not have complete control over their investment. Unlike factory-built products, and as we shall see in Chapter 3, even commodified celebrities have minds of their own and the capacity for independent action.

From the celebrity's point of view, their personal objective is most likely to be the construction of a viable career through the astute distribution and regulation of the sales of their celebrity-commodity (Turner et al., 2000: 13). Celebrity is typically short-lived and so for this to occur celebrities need advice about how to market themselves – much in the way a manufacturing business will use specialists to help them develop a marketing plan, a system for modifying and improving the product, and a strategy for building and maintaining consumer loyalty (Gamson, 1994: 58). While this will involve acknowledging that their commodified status must generate some personal costs along the way, the aim is to trade as a celebrity-commodity in order to produce benefits for the individual. This, in turn, involves the careful choice of strategies that will increase the value of this commodity to the industry and to third party intermediaries, without sacrificing those aspects of the celebrity's existence they see as crucial to their personal happiness.[2]

The web of conflicting interests embedded in this situation has been no impediment to its expansion. The marketing of, and the markets for, celebrity have increased dramatically over the last few decades. The key to this process may lie in how interdependent these competing interests have become, as the structures of celebrity and the media industries today co-exist in 'a kind of twisted symbiosis' (Giles, 2000: 26) that is perfectly reflected in the media's effective incorporation of a growing and increasingly rationalised paparazzi industry (McNamara, 2011). The celebrity (and, indeed, the public) may well deplore how cynically this industry feeds the public interest in their private lives, and how personally intrusive its effects can be. However, it is this public interest which can also attract people to see their next film or their next live appearance. That expression of interest, in turn, provides them with the power to elicit an adulatory photo feature in *Hello!* or to demand approval of the writer assigned to prepare a profile on them for *Vanity Fair* – all of which will go towards enhancing the cultural capital invested in their public image. For the magazine editors concerned, these photos and that feature will sell magazines. The public demand for material on A-list celebrities means that the media (particularly the magazines) must assiduously maintain access to them; the price for this – once the celebrity concerned achieves a certain level of fame – may be to accede to whatever conditions the celebrity proposes.[3] Conversely, since the celebrity in turn will always need the visibility the media can provide, it is in their interests to be as cooperative as possible to maintain a continuing relationship. As a result they will provide images free of charge to the magazines, they will appear at publicity events to promote this year's new television series, they will do the round of talk shows to promote their next tour, and so on.

In a similar network of coordinated but competing interests, the film producer will contract the star to advertise and promote their film as well as perform in it. This is to maximise the visibility and appeal of the film so that it makes a profit for the production company. While they may desire that outcome as well, the star's personal interests here are slightly different. The star promotes their latest work as a means of enhancing their commercial value in general, and so it is possible that they will be reluctant to closely tie this publicity to the particular performance vehicle. Gamson suggests that 'the performer who wants to increase her marketability as a celebrity persona', may be 'resistant to the link to work' (that is, the film they are publicising), preferring to promote their personality alone (1994: 84). As Barry King has pointed out, the film actor has little choice but to commodify themselves in this way. There are not enough parts to go around and very little money is paid to those who are not in high demand. As a result, says King, 'competition for parts, *given the operation of naturalistic conventions*, lead to an emphasis on what is unique to the actor, displacing emphasis from what an actor can do *qua* actor onto what the actor *qua* person or biographical entity is' (King, 1991: 178). The construction of a star persona may result in some 'loss of autonomy' (ibid.: 180) in terms of the constraints on their off-screen life and their professional choices, but this is regarded as a reasonable trade-off for increased market power within the industry. A similar pattern can be seen elsewhere. In her account of the rock music industry, Deena Weinstein explains why there is a focus there too upon the individual rather than 'the work': 'If record companies can get listeners to fall in love with the person rather than the song, there's a better chance fans will buy the next album – and concert ticket, T-shirt, video, book and poster' (1999: 65). Joe Moran's account of changes in literary publishing notes the recent expansion of forms of publicity that concentrate on the author (talk shows, feature articles and so on), as well as the increasing investment in celebrity authors for publisher-generated projects. You can get some sense of the scale and focus of this kind of investment by noting that so far Susan Boyle has been the subject of two biographies and one autobiography, David Hasselhoff has written two autobiographies, and Justin Bieber has already been the subject of five biographies and one autobiography! Promoting authors as personalities is a defining symptom of the integration of literary production into the entertainment industry (Moran, 2000: 41).

While most parts of the celebrity industry would probably prefer to operate like more conventional manufacturing industries – producing a standardised product in the way a factory production-line might – the whole structure of celebrity is built on the construction of the individuated personality. In practice, the individual star has a highly identifiable, even iconic, physical image, a specific history for the circulation of this image, and accrues psychological and semiotic depth over time (De Cordova, 1990: 9). The interests of the individual seeking celebrity are overwhelmingly in favour of pursuing that kind of specificity, what David Marshall discusses as the managed or motivated performance of the celebrity's 'persona'. However, in the media and entertainment industries' version of the ideal world, their interests would be better served if they could be guaranteed a steady supply of less specific, more formulaic, interchangeable celebrity-commodities. These would not mature as capital assets and thus increase production costs, and the market value of any one identity would be not much different to any other. While the studios of the classic Hollywood era probably offer the best example of this principle in practice, it is not surprising to find that some sectors of the contemporary media have also organised themselves to produce celebrities along these lines.

Certain teenage stars in television soap operas, for instance, enjoy a high level of visibility in the USA, the UK and Australia (among other locations), but in many cases find that once they leave the serial they are unable to find other work. They are easily replaced and quickly forgotten. In the research conducted for *Fame Games* (Turner et al., 2000), my co-authors and I found that a number of the former stars of Australian soap operas such as *Neighbours* and *Home and Away* were no longer working in the industry because they simply had no credibility as an actor once they had left their original roles. Their celebrity was built on their exposure in a particular, low-prestige vehicle and maximised through an industrial structure that vigorously exploited cross-media and multi-platform promotions. (In the case of the most successful teen soap operas in Australia, the television network that commissioned the production owned the only national television guide magazine, as well as most of the market leaders in the women's magazine sector. Soap stars were routinely featured on their covers as well as in features across this sector.) Once they left the series, however, they were easily replaced on all these platforms by the next cast of fresh young faces.

The rise in popularity of reality TV formats making use of 'ordinary people' (Turner, 2010) as participants is responsible for what has become currently the most firmly established industrial pattern for the production of these disposable celebrities. We now have reality TV stars, a key example of Rojek's 'celetoid', as they move from maximum visibility (on our television screens every night, and in our newspapers and magazines in the morning) to complete obscurity within a matter of weeks. Reality TV formats, from *Big Brother* to *Idol* to game-docs such as *The Amazing Race,* are designed to produce a reliable supply of interchangeable celebrities for the format to deliver to the television audience. The supply of participants for these programmes seems inexhaustible even though it is clear to everyone involved that whatever celebrity achieved is most likely bound to be short-lived. Not only is this fundamental to the design of the format, but also in many cases it is reinforced by the contractual arrangements between the production company and participants (Turner, 2010). Just as it was for the young actor in the daily soaps, it is very difficult (if not impossible) for the individual 'housemate', contestant, or participant to develop the level of control over their public persona that is required to maintain a relationship with the audience which is independent of the programme – that is, a relationship that is not managed by the production company or the network.[4]

The production companies are aware of this situation, but largely find no ethical problem with it: in most cases, the persons concerned might be considered lucky to last as long as they do. Those who do find it a little uncomfortable are the agents, managers and publicists who have become integrated into the celebrity's life, and who have to some extent identified with the long-term objective of their survival as a public figure. For these people, the interests of the industry and those of the individual come into conflict in ways that create practical, strategic dilemmas. To what extent do they encourage the young reality TV star to unburden themselves of intimate personal information in an interview, for instance, knowing that this could haunt them for the rest of their career (or, more crucially, the rest of their lives)? Similarly, to what extent do they support the celebrity's intention of providing revealing photographs as a way of heightening their short-term visibility when the agents know that these could well limit their charge's career options down the track? The metaphor of 'celebrity-commodity' that we have been using contains within it the contradictions the industry deals with every day: the fact that commercial interests may well run contrary to the personal interests of the celebrity.

This is even more of a concern when we look at the effect of media interest in the 'accidental celebrity' – the person in the news – such as Princess Diana's former butler, Paul Burrell. As a result of the court case in which he was involved, he became a celebrity-commodity for a very short time and seems to have been advised to cash in as fully and as quickly as possible. In Burrell's case, this meant selling his story to one mass circulation newspaper for a large sum (despite having earlier claimed he would never try to make money out of his association with Diana). Those newspapers who did not win the auction for his story were free to attack him and the paper that did secure the story – by ridiculing Burrell, undermining his credibility, seeking new information to embarrass him, and challenging the details of his story and so on. As the subsequent physical attacks on Burrell's home have demonstrated, the acceptance of celebrity-commodity status can carry quite severe personal consequences. It involves a framework of behaviour over which the individual will have virtually no control. In our research for *Fame Games* (Turner et al., 2000), Frances Bonner, David Marshall and I examined the media representation of one such individual – Stuart Diver, the lone survivor of a catastrophic landslide in the Australian snowfields. The only way such a person could control their media representation was by fully engaging with the celebrity industries that produced it: by hiring a manager and surrendering control of the situation to a media professional who would entirely commercialise all media access. Apparently, Stuart Diver regarded this as an ethically objectionable thing to do (it could appear to be an attempt to cash in on the misfortunes of others), but he was persuaded that this was the only realistic course available to him – and it worked. The provision of exclusive access to one media organisation terminated the interest of the others; they did not want to publicise a competitor's property and in this case they were not interested in turning on a figure who had become a hero to the public.

Once achieved, of course, celebrity can spin off into many related sub-industries through endorsements, merchandising and the like. Individuals can become brands in their own right, with enormous commercial potential. McDonald and Andrews report that one year after signing Michael Jordan for Gatorade's 'Be like Mike' promotion, Gatorade's annual revenues had increased from $681 million to over $1 billion (2001: 20). Increasingly, the worldwide marketing of such figures as Michael Jordan has served to expand America's penetration into global markets, especially in film, television and video. In sport, though, this has been a relatively recent development.

David Rowe (1995) argues that before the 1970s there was nothing chic or fashionable about sport or sports stars. However, a shift in the cultural and economic location of sport resulted in the increased marketing of sports stars as commodities. The growing sophistication of televised sport has enhanced their visibility and their cultural purchase. Further, the cultural and industrial convergence of sport and fashion is a particularly interesting development that seems to have exercised an exceptionally strong influence on the role of the sports star. Whannel (2002) describes how functional sporting attire like the tracksuit and the sports shoe became stylised fashion items as the mainstream fashion industry borrowed from sports styles. More notable, perhaps, is the growth of what Whannel describes as 'fitness chic' (ibid.: 129–32): the extraordinary rise in the popularity of fitness clubs and the 'exercise boom' that began in the 1990s and has continued unabated into the present. The degree of market penetration achieved by sports goods brands using these stars can be seen in the ubiquity of sports brands in department stores and clothing shops today. Where once we might have seen a range of commercial logos on the t-shirts on sale in mainstream fashion outlets, today the market is dominated by designer names and sports-goods logos – Nike, Puma, Adidas, Reebok, Converse and so on. All of these developments have generated a relatively new intensity to the media's focus on the appearance, style and personality of the sports star in their behaviour off the track. As a result, sports people too are 'celebrated and exploited':

> It is their labour and performance that is minutely scrutinized and whose skills are bought and sold in the sporting marketplace, their bodies which are punished, manipulated and invaded in the quest for greater efficiency, and their images moulded and displayed to sell and promote goods and services. (Whannel, 2002: 113)

According to Rein et al. (1997), sports stars can now expect to earn up to two-thirds of their annual income through product endorsements of various kinds – ranging from the tools of their trade (sports shoes, tennis racquets, etc.) to food lines (yoghurt, breakfast cereals) and fashion items (clothing, sunglasses and so on). The highest rating sports star in the Forbes Celebrity 100, Tiger Woods (he comes in at No. 12), even after losing tens of millions of dollars in endorsements after his messy divorce, was estimated to be earning between $50–$60 million in endorsements over 2012.

The final point to note about the celebrity-commodity is the close relationship between celebrity and the consumption of commodities. We have already seen how David Marshall's work maps the function celebrity performs in linking ideologies of individualism, consumerism and democratic capitalism. De Cordova's history of film stardom discusses the way that film stars operated as a means of promoting the values of consumerism during the 1920s and 1930s. Drawing on Larry May's research, he argues that the ideological work to be accomplished there was to negotiate the tensions between 'Victorian ideals and consumer ideals' as part of the process of the commodification of everyday life. Film stars were a good place for this negotiation to occur. They were not excessively privileged in terms of their social power, they came largely from ordinary socio-economic backgrounds, and their success was 'easily ascribed to democratic aspirations. In conspicuously displaying that success through material possessions, the star vividly demonstrated the idea that satisfaction was not to be found in work but in one's activities away from work – in consumption and leisure' (De Cordova, 1990: 108). The demonstration continues today, when celebrities promote their latest venture in a leisure location – by the hotel pool, at home, in a restaurant, or on the golf course. The consumerist values they work to legitimate are also fundamental to the commercial interests of the media outlets. As Conboy says in relation to the news media's use of celebrity, 'one of the attractions of celebrity news is that it allows the people as readers to be addressed and articulated in terms of consumerist values which are inextricably linked to the newspapers' economic agenda' (2002: 150). Stories routinely present the celebrity as a model of consumption practice and aspiration for the reader. The usual ambiguities still appear, of course. While these stories can represent the commodity consumption of the celebrity as spectacular and exorbitant, they can also use their consumer behaviour as a means of constructing their everydayness – their similarity to 'us'.

THE CELEBRITY INDUSTRIES

In this section I want to outline some of the structures of the celebrity industry, beginning with the function of the third parties mentioned earlier: the agents, managers, and publicists. That might seem a rudimentary way to begin, but it is information that rarely finds its way into analysis of the production of celebrity, or of the wealth of texts this production process employs. This is especially damaging in this particular instance because the celebrity industries actively mask their own activities. By presenting publicity as news, by claiming to tell us what their charges 'are really like', by managing the production of 'candid' photo opportunities and so on, the celebrity industries work hard to naturalise their professional practices – or else to submerge their professional practices beneath those of another profession, such as journalism. As a result, what these industries do is not easy to distinguish and therefore their importance is not easy to assess. Currently, there are very few studies available that approach the topic from this angle – to analyse this industry in the way you might want to analyse the film industry or the television production industry. Joshua Gamson's *Claims to Fame* (1994), Marshall's *Celebrity and Power* (1997) and Rein et al.'s *High Visibility* (1997) are probably the most useful and recent books dealing with the American industry, and the work of Frances Bonner, David Marshall and myself in *Fame Games* (Turner et al., 2000) provides an account of a much smaller and less organised industry. More recently, Chris Rojek's *Fame Attack* (2012) has focused in particular on the fundamental role played by the invention of public relations in the development of the celebrity industry in general. This section of the chapter will draw on these works extensively.

Let us start with what Rein et al. (1997) call the 'structure of the celebrity industry'. I should point out that their book deals solely with the American industry and responds to an expansion of the techniques of celebrity marketing into politics, business, academia and religion that is certainly more developed there than in any other country. There will be variations from the model they outline – and I will deal with these later in the chapter – but it is useful to focus on America as it still has the most developed version of the celebrity industry (from my observation, the UK media is probably the most obsessive about celebrity, but its obsession is highly concentrated within the tabloid print media). Unlike most other accounts, Rein et al.

locate the celebrity industry in the centre of an industrial structure, rather than as an ancillary to it. According to their point of view, it is the entertainment and sports industries that are on the fringe of the celebrity industry, not the other way round. Their justification for this point of view lies in the pervasiveness of the techniques of celebrity (marketing, public relations and publicity) across so many sectors of the economy.

As they describe it, the celebrity industry is supported by eight contributing 'sub-industries'. The activity of these sub-industries is not solely dedicated to the celebrity industry, but Rein et al. describe the celebrity industry as coordinating the services the sub-industries provide in order to produce and promote the celebrity. The first industry they nominate, predictably enough, is the *entertainment industry*, incorporating theatre, music halls, dance halls, sports arenas and movie studios. They differentiate these from the *communications industry*, which encompasses newspapers, magazines, radio, television and film. The activities of both the entertainment and communications industries are promoted through the *publicity industry*, which comprises publicists, PR firms, advertising agencies and marketing research firms. The celebrities themselves are handled by the *representation industry*, which includes agents, personal managers and promoters. The production of the celebrity image is coordinated through the *appearance industry*, which includes costumers, cosmeticians, hairstylists and other kinds of image consultants. The professional performance is dealt with by the *coaching industry* – music, dance, speech and modelling teachers. Finally, we have the *endorsement industry* – souvenir manufacturers, clothing manufacturers and games and toys manufacturers among others – and the *legal and business services industry*, which provides legal, accounting and investment advice (Rein et al., 1997: 42–58).

We don't need to accept these categories, of course, but they do give us a good overview of the range of cultural intermediaries required to make this system function, although it underplays the role of public relations (see Rojek, 2012). It also leaves out of the picture what Gamson regards as a key industrial element of the celebrity system: While he also acknowledges the roles of 'paid specialists' who 'surround the celebrities to increase and protect their market value', he also points to 'the linked sub-industries' that 'make use of celebrities for their own commercial purposes, simultaneously building and using performers' attention-getting power' (1994: 61). The whole edifice of commercial branding that Naomi Klein has described in *No Logo* (2000) – an edifice which is certainly larger than the 'endorsement industry' but that is fundamentally concerned with the use of celebrity images – is not entirely contained by the structure presented to us in Rein et al.'s *High Visibility*.[5]

So, while we must acknowledge that the pervasiveness of celebrity affects our ability to neatly describe the structure of the industry that produces it, these categories provide something of a starting point. Gamson (1994), Turner et al. (2000) and Rein et al. (1997) all provide detailed outlines of the practices and processes performed by the specialists in the celebrity industry: the differences between the roles played by agents and managers, the range of duties performed by the publicist and so on. There is no need to duplicate their work here. However, it is worth briefly reviewing the nature of the roles played by, in particular, the key figures within the representation and publicity industries – agents, managers and publicists. There will be some variations, from market to market, so largely what follows is an account of the American model; where the model varies, in the UK and elsewhere, this will be flagged as we go along.

The role of what was originally called the press agent goes back quite a way, and is described at length in Gabler's (1995) biography of Walter Winchell. Appearing around the end of the nineteenth century to exploit the potential for free publicity provided by an expanding print media, they took off as a profession during the 1920s and 1930s. Largely their role then was to locate items in gossip columns such as Winchell's, in return for a fee paid by their client. Widely despised, they constituted 'an unsavoury and forlorn group of men', according to Gabler, but were nevertheless 'the ants that moved the mountain. For without them, there was no celebrity, no gossip, no mass culture, really' (1995: 249). Certainly, it is from their early occupation of the market in celebrity gossip and entertainment industry publicity that they laid the ground for the subsequent development of the industry from the 1920s to the 1950s. Industrial structures that had developed around theatre and vaudeville were modified to accommodate new means of production and publicity, with the expansion of the print media's coverage of their activities. The theatrical agent's activities crossed over into the film industry as it expanded and the development of television created a demand for network publicists and public relations personnel, as well as a major new outlet for promotional and publicity material. In sport, as we have seen already, the arrival of the agent was much later than in the entertainment industry. 'Sports attorneys' appear in the 1970s to prosecute the interests of the players in gaining access to a fairer share of the revenues from elite sport – particularly those generated by television where the appeal of the individual sports star was of major importance.

The agent in the entertainment industry, in general, is there to find work for their clients, to help negotiate the terms of that work, to provide advice and sometimes developmental coaching, and – in certain cases – to arrange publicity for the client. Successful agents will have a large number of clients and operate on a percentage cut of the client's fee. Mostly they will not interest themselves in management or 'product development'. Indeed, it is not really in their interests to become too closely identified with a particular client because their value to the industry is as a conduit to many possible performers, not just one. Agents thus tend to have a close relationship with the employers of their clients – the booking agents, casting directors and so on. This can lead to conflicts of interest, where the agent is a little too keen to find someone for the casting agency and pushes their client into an inappropriate commitment. In sports, the agent tends to have a slightly different role, although in many respects even more conflicted. They tend to operate as the middle man in the whole enterprise, 'handling economic relations between individual sports stars, sports organisations, sponsors, advertisers, and television companies' (Rowe, 1995: 112). This is similar to the role played in other sectors by the personal manager.

The manager typically has a smaller number of clients and plays a much larger strategic role in developing their careers. The management service they provide is extraordinarily comprehensive, organising their clients' whole lives: 'answering their mail, investing their money, buying real estate, planning their schedules, placing their children in schools, even hiring the gardener and firing the maid' (Rein et al., 1997: 46). In some cases, both in the American studies and in the work we completed in Australia, the power of the manager developed to the point where they also had a media profile equivalent to that of most celebrities. Impresario managers with their own entrepreneurial projects tend to emerge from this kind of system: Michael Ovitz in the USA, Max Clifford in the UK, and Harry M. Miller in Australia are examples of this.

Public relations is an industry barely a century old and the carrier of a slightly tarnished reputation. This wasn't always the case. Indeed, initially, public relations provided a more respectable name for the press agent as well as the rationale for a change in the function of these operatives: the need for positive publicity gradually became a corporate issue, not just a problem for the entertainment industries. These days, public relations touches most facets of commercial and public life: managing corporate relations with the public, providing advice to politicians about how to build their public image, designing a government public information campaign, or managing mass media controversies to protect the interests of their clients. In many quarters, this has lent public relations a reputation for massaging the truth through the media. Among the reasons for this has been the tendency for businesses or politicians caught in an embarrassing situation to deal with it by commissioning a public relations company rather than by addressing the situation directly.

As Rojek describes it in *Fame Attack* (2012), the development of public relations and the underpinning philosophy of its founder, Edward Bernays, lies at the centre of the celebrity industry. Public relations or PR is frequently used as the generic term to describe, perjoratively, the operation of publicity, media management and 'spin' – even though many of the actual activities involved are likely to be carried out by promotions personnel or publicity officers. In the celebrity industry, public relations operatives may be employed by organisations with continuing interests to protect – studios, networks, production companies and so on – but they tend not to get involved in the day-to-day operation of the publicity and promotion of individuals. To some extent this is a hierarchical distinction: although publicity is a sub-section of public relations, many in PR look down on the crudely commercial work required by publicity and promotion. From another point of view, however, it simply recognises the greater industrial importance of the publicist to the celebrity and media industries.

Publicists may be hired by the celebrity, by their management, by a specialist publicity or public relations firm, or by the production unit, network or promoter involved with the celebrity's current project. They stand between the celebrity and the public, almost literally, in that their job is to manage all communications between them. They write the press releases and secure their placement; they stage-manage the photo opportunity that will feature at the end of the evening news and orchestrate any personal appearances the celebrity performs; they negotiate with magazine editors about how their client will be represented in a photo-shoot and feature article; they will vet the questions asked by journalists and television interviewers, and sit with their client while the interview takes place to ensure that it follows the established rules of engagement. Often, they will impersonate their celebrity client on Twitter, compose the posts onto the official website, and respond to comments from the fans. They will deal with the press when their client misbehaves and attracts negative publicity – hoping to cash in on their ongoing relationship with the press to minimise any fall-out. The publicist's function is to control, coordinate, and if necessary massage that information and those images of the celebrity which are circulated to the public. This can involve frustrating the desires of the celebrity they represent, as well as those of the media outlets expecting to have their demands satisfied. The successful publicist's value lies in their ability to do all this while maintaining effective relationships with those on both sides of the transaction. This is possible because what I am describing as controlling can also be seen as enabling: while they exercise a powerful influence on what kind of transaction actually takes place, they are also the mechanism that organises it and thus enables it to happen at all. That said, and as we shall see in the next chapter, their effectiveness may well be one of the reasons for celebrities choosing to make direct personal use of the capacities of social media such as Twitter precisely in order to bypass these intermediaries, to communicate more directly with their fans, or to attempt to unilaterally create a more authentic persona (Marshall, 2010).

Notwithstanding this development, and as remarked upon earlier, the key to the structure of the industry is the especially close pattern of economic interdependencies that bind the celebrity and their representatives (agents, managers, publicists, PR people) to the entertainment industries and the entertainment and news media. The most obvious connections are corporate – such as when we find that *Time* magazine is featuring a story on an actor who is currently appearing in a film produced by Warner Bros. – but there are others: strong social, cultural and professional networks see individuals move easily from one side of the industrial divide to the other, and so reporters become press officers, journalists become public relations advisers, and so on. These networks are supported by a transactional pattern that will see a front page story traded for exclusive access so that both the star and the media outlet achieve their professional goals. These interdependencies are, in my view, deliberately mystified so that the processes through which they work – how a news story on a celebrity finds its way to the front page for instance – are not visible. This serves two sets of interests: those of the publicist, who wants the items published to appear as news rather than as advertising because it will be more credible; and those of the journalist, who does not wish their readers to know that the item under their byline was not the product of the practice of journalism. Neither of these positions is particularly ethically secure and so they are not maintained without tension. They accompany what seems to be a constant battle for power.

PUBLICITY, NEWS AND POWER

British journalist, Toby Young (2001), has written about his experience of working for the American glossy magazine *Vanity Fair* in the 1990s. With a background in a chic variety of journalism in the UK (he co-edited *Modern Review* with Julie Burchill), Young was attracted to the prestige of *Vanity Fair* for a short-term position he hoped would turn into something more permanent. It was his first experience of the heartland of celebrity journalism, however, and his book is dominated by his ambivalent attitude to what he saw. While Young admits to being seduced by celebrity to the point where he would do almost anything to gain admittance to one of the elite celebrity events, he also expresses concern at the power wielded by the publicists charged with advancing the interests of A-list celebrities:

> I was particularly shocked by the extent to which the glossy magazines have given up their right to free speech in return for access to celebrities. Thanks to the antics of women like Pat Kingsley [the head of one of the most important agencies, PMK], the power of PRs to control what's written about their clients is now absolute. On one famous occasion, Kingsley rejected fourteen writers before deciding on one who was deferential enough to interview Tom Cruise for *Rolling Stone*.[6] (2001: 333)

He understands the reason, though, which is systemic. As he puts it, the 'PRs have them [the editors] by the short and curlies. In order to sell their magazines on the news-stands, the editors need to get A-list stars to pose for their covers and the only way to do that is to agree to whatever terms the publicists dictate' (ibid.: 110). As the media industries have converged, so have the supporting networks – and this has an effect on their market power as well. Young points to the 2001 merger between Pat Kingsley's agency PMK and their largest rival Huvane Baum Halls, which resulted in 'virtually the whole of the Hollywood A-list being represented by one company under the control of Pat Kingsley' (ibid.: 110). The market power her company would hold as a result of this would be irresistible.

This is a familiar complaint: that what is now a structurally embedded relationship between the news media and the publicity arm of the celebrity industry compromises the independence of the news media and its capacity to simply tell the truth as it sees it – or just run the stories it wants to and that it thinks its audiences might want to read. It accompanies the observation that celebrity material has inserted itself increasingly into our media diet and that this is the result of the increasing power of publicity. Celebrity gossip dominates the mass magazine market, for instance, and it has changed the content of television news. Rein et al. (1997: 286) claim that 70 per cent of all information that is published as news originates in publicity and public relations. This kind of claim is made so consistently across markets (Turner, Bonner and Marshall generated similar figures for Australia in *Fame Games* [2000] and Bob Franklin makes a similar claim about the UK in *Newzsak* [1997]), that any contemporary discussion of the production of news which does not seriously assess the importance of the contributions of publicists and PR personnel must be inadequate. I am aware that journalists themselves often deny such an influence but these denials simply fly in the face of a welter of evidence to the contrary.

A slightly different complaint concerns those media formats regarded as serving an informational function for their audiences but which have been captured by publicity and PR. News is not the only one to be nominated here. The talk-show interview, for instance, which began as a 'means of revelation', is now just another location for the exercise of 'image-control' (Gamson, 1994: 47). Rather than telling us why Hugh Grant committed that indiscretion with a prostitute in LA, his appearance on Jay Leno's show was designed to convince his audience that he was, after all, just a 'nice guy'. Those who have used this tactic for renovating a public persona include Mel Gibson, Russell Brand, Tom Cruise, Britney Spears, Mariah Carey, and most dramatically in recent times, disgraced Tour de France cyclist, Lance Armstrong, in his much publicised interview with Oprah in 2013. Even those media platforms that might have looked as if they would work in the public's favour, then, have been surrendered to the industry, or as David Chaney has put it: 'the supplementary industries of being interviewed, pictured, described, explained are not a bridge between audiences and public figures, they are the ways in which personalities are constituted and sustained' (1993: 144). This is not a matter of infiltration, or of disproportionate influence; it is a repurposing of the media format itself.

Of course, publicists are not just manipulative, they are also useful. They share daily professional routines with entertainment journalists in particular and know what their needs are. They can supply angles on stories, quotes, pictures and artwork, background information, contacts and networking opportunities. They 'find, mould, and provide precisely what the media covering them need' (Gamson, 1994: 86), and in the end they might wind up, effectively, writing the story in their press release. Journalists, of course, agonise over this. What started out as a fairly straightforward enlistment in the practice of independent and objective journalism has becomes a professionalised process of informally negotiated compromise. Worse still, their access to information depends on the success of these informal but nevertheless professional negotiations and so there is little room for them to move. What Gamson calls 'mutual co-optation' does not only affect the moral purity of the participants, however; it also influences a preference for the publishing of those pieces approved by the publicist – towards the publishing of 'fluff' (ibid.: 88–9), the light gossipy pieces that offend neither party to the transaction. As one of Gamson's sources puts it: 'It's nobody's ambition to be generating these kinds of things, but we can't get away from it. They sell.' (ibid.: 89).

While the infiltration of publicity into news production is widespread, the power relations that structure the gatekeeping operation do vary from place to place. Young's account, for instance, makes explicit comparison with the situation in the UK, where, he claims, the publicists have nothing like the level of influence they enjoy in the United States. The supply of celebrities is differently organised there, of course, and the particular version of 'attack dog journalism' practised by the British tabloid newspapers makes them objects of fear for most celebrities and their minders (hence the intensity of their fury when the *News of the World* phone-hacking scandal erupted). However, there is also a slightly different ideological frame as well. According to Young's account, where the American journalist was seduced by proximity to fame and therefore sought to get ever closer to the world of celebrity, the relationship between the British 'hacks and flacks' was 'essentially adversarial' (2001: 107). PRs were 'the enemy' and those who were caught up in the scene they were covering were branded 'social climbers' and 'mistrusted by their colleagues'. 'In some vague, undefined way, to get too chummy with the kind of people who appear in *Hello!*', Young writes, 'is regarded as a betrayal of the hack warrior's code' (ibid.: 112).

One imagines that a similar point of view would be taken by those who work in American tabloids such as *The National Enquirer* and *Us Week*, celebrity sites such as *TMZ*, or by bloggers such as Perez Hilton. Like the British tabloids they refuse to play by any cosy, relationship-building rules, as their audience wants to see the sleazy, shocking exposé that publicists have nightmares about, not the benign and bland output of other sections of the celebrity industry. Often, the items published in these outlets are provided by amateur informants or sourced off the internet, which now hosts many alternative sources (professional, amateur and pro-am) of celebrity gossip, dedicated to undermining that provided by the publicity industry. Most of the images for these magazines come from the international paparazzi who have become so commercially necessary to the industry – supplying the demand for new images – that they have now become a mini-industry in their own right (McNamara, 2011).[7] Even though their alleged role in Princes Diana's death confirmed their pariah status for the public, the paparazzi now operate in an increasingly corporatised manner to provide the raw material for the celebrity industry. There remains, nonetheless, a guerilla element to this oppositional component of the media's coverage of celebrity, which might make it appear to run counter to the interests of the industry itself. Even so, it also works to further intensify the cultural visibility and purchase of celebrity as a commodity. The more respectable media outlets, with their highly convergent industrial structure and their investment in cross-media and cross-platform promotions, largely concentrate on satisfying one dimension of the audience's interest in celebrity – their function as objects of admiration and desire. But another sector of the media, perhaps even larger in scale if not in public visibility, satisfies the equally important alternative interest – in the celebrity's function as the object of derision, ridicule and resentment. Alongside *Hello!* and *Vanity Fair* on the news-stand are *People, Now, The National Enquirer,* and the various national franchises of magazines such as *FHM.* Their attitude to the celebrity industry can be anything but respectful, focusing on scandals and embarrassing paparazzi shots, and surrounding them with a rich vein of bitchy and ironic captions and headers. Many are free to take this attitude simply because they are not dependent upon continuing relationships with the publicists. Further, they are sufficiently successful in the marketplace to succeed without making deals of the kind that so shocked Toby Young – indeed, their appeal lies in their scurrilousness and their disinterest in printing benign 'fluff'. Much of what they print may be regarded as *malign* fluff, but it addresses a set of audience interests that are neglected by the majority of the respectable media.

As the very existence of these magazines demonstrates, and despite all the professional investment in image control, the system still doesn't work perfectly in the publicity industries' interests. Just as well, because much of the audience does not want it to. Among the appeals of celebrity journalism is its revelation of the scandalous, the bizarre, the pathetic, the phony, the disturbing and the gross. Hugh Grant is arrested in the back seat of his car with a prostitute, Michael Jackson dangles his baby off a hotel balcony, Britney Spears is photographed having her head shaved, Tiger Woods admits to 'sex addiction', and Justin Bieber vomits in mid-performance on stage. On the one hand, then, the ultimate challenge to the power of the publicist can often be the person they are publicising and they must do everything they can to keep them under control. On the other hand, from the audience's point of view there is an intrinsic interest in the kinds of moments that occur when the publicist loses that control. Not only do they remind us that these celebrities are not especially gifted at managing their lives, but they also provide us with entertaining narratives to follow through the news. Such pleasures are among the fundamental attractions to the representations of celebrity in popular culture.

As a commercial enterprise, the celebrity industry must serve competing industrial interests while, as a cultural production, satisfying radically contradictory demands from consumers. As a result, the celebrity industry may be organised but it is not particularly coherent. Much of what it does, obsessively, it does on a hunch. In his research for *Fame Games* (Turner, Bonner and Marshall, 2000), David Marshall talked to a television network executive who, during the 1980s, had the job of protecting *Neighbours* stars Jason Donovan and Kylie Minogue from the news of their romantic relationship becoming public. This was a major task for the network publicity people for a period of four years. The reason for this was the firmly held assumption that the *Neighbours* audience figures would be negatively affected if the truth was published. There was never any research conducted to test this assumption, but it operated with the power of fact in the network's strategy for years. This highlights a key point that Joshua Gamson makes: one of the reasons for the publicity industries' excessive anxiety about media management and control is the lack of knowledge about what will actually succeed in the marketplace, about what audiences actually want. While the television industry will closely watch its ratings and sometimes the TVQ scores, and while film producers routinely test their films before preview audiences, the industrial system that is focused on producing and marketing the celebrity actually pays very little attention to the audience. Instead it is taken for granted that audience interest is reflected in a high level of public visibility – hence the obsession with media coverage:

> [p]ublicists use the *perception* of audience interest as a signal to industry buyers that their client has a reliable market. They do so by bypassing audiences, using the more controllable media coverage as a proxy for audience interest ... [T]he working assumption is that media institutions are in touch with and reflect audience interest. As long as that assumption is maintained by entertainment industry buyers, publicity workers can operate without requiring more knowledge about audiences. (Gamson, 1994: 111)

There is an operational strategy, then, for considering the audience's interest, but this strategy does little more than simply play back to publicists the effects of their own labour. Publicists would rarely conduct audience research on their celebrity's marketability. Little wonder that one of the talkshow producers Gamson interviews about the basis upon which he decides the line-up of guests on his show admits that, on the whole, 'we don't know shit' about audiences (ibid.: 115).

Gary Whannel also points out that despite the amount of time invested in controlling media visibility, there is a point where media events build up a momentum of their own. At such points the celebrity industry also becomes an onlooker, as what he calls 'the vortex of publicity' exceeds the capacity of the economy of production:

> The growth in the range of media outlets, and the vastly increased speed of circulation of information have combined to create a phenomenon of a 'vortex' effect, which I term here 'vortextuality'. The various media constantly feed off each other and, in an era of electronic and digital information exchange, the speed at which this happens can be very rapid. Certain major super-events come to dominate the headlines to such an extent that it becomes temporarily difficult for columnists or commentators to discuss anything else. (2002: 206)

The instance he cites is of course the death of Princess Diana, which created a 'short-term compression of the media agenda in which other topics either disappear or have to be connected to the vortextual event' (ibid.: 206).

Given the conflict of interests structured into the industry, the gaps in its understanding of the context in which it is operating and the capacity for media coverage to become an event with a momentum of its own, it is not surprising that there are certain limits to the power of the celebrity industry. At times there is little it can do to extricate itself from a situation, or to determine how it will play out. When that happens, the same media who have grudgingly (but silently) honoured their deals with the devil of PR are only too happy to write a feature for the *Los Angeles Times* or the *Guardian* about the regrettable operation of 'spin' and its threat to the public's right to know.

NOTES

1 The names of these companies tend to change a lot, as mergers result in new labels being devised. For a good account of the most recent situation, and the concentration of interests, see Hesmondhalgh (2013: Chapter 6).
2 Richard Dyer's *Heavenly Bodies* (1986) provides us with three case studies of stars who rebelled against their commodification and whose personal lives were forfeited as a result of their loss of control over the circulation and definition of their image.
3 As David Giles (2000: 137)) points out in relation to the music press, the magazine's readers' 'loyalty lies less with the publication than with a single band or artist', and so the music journalist's relationship with the stars is 'permanently on a knife-edge'.
4 There are exceptions to this rule, of course, with successful contestants on *Idol* such as Kelly Clarkson going on to build a career, and with unlikely and apparently talentless participants such as William Hung (from *American Idol*) and Jade Goody (from serial *Big Brothers*) providing key examples.
5 It is hard to find a category, too, for more diverse and obscure activities, such as the celebrity tracking services (for a hefty fee you can commission tracking reports on your favourite celebrity's whereabouts), the directories of personal image consultants marketed to everyday people as well as to celebrities, celebrity look-alike agencies, and the new career category of 'celebrity assistants'.
6 I suspect this story has an apochryphal dimension to it: Gamson quotes it too but he says Kingsley vetted 20 writers before she was satisfied! Friend's (2002) newspaper feature cites it as well, and gives the figure as 14.
7 While legendary paparazzi like Phil Ramey continue to haunt the stars, Ken Mazur gives us the latest version of the freelance photographer: he runs a stable of 600 celebrity photographers through his company WireImage. What makes Mazur and his staff different is that they coordinate their activities with 'the marketing and publicity interests of our corporate clients' – the celebrities themselves (Sales, 2003). Candid photos are guaranteed to align with the image development

interests of the promotions and publicity industries. Kim McNamara (2011: 522) has outlined how the paparazzi industry has mutated from being a service to the print media to being a media presence in its own right – setting up agency websites and leaving the streets behind. Further, agencies such as Splash and Big Pictures have adjunct sites where 'citizen paparazzi' can sell their pictures to the agency (ibid.: 523). 'Paparazzi sites', she says, 'are starting to resemble a hybrid of social networking and entertainment sites, simultaneously bringing news to audiences and reaping it from them' (ibid.: 527).

3 Manufacturing Celebrity

Fame used to be a by-product. [Now] it's like 'What do you want to be when you grow up?' 'Famous.' 'What for?' 'It doesn't matter.'

(Pop diva Kylie Minogue, talking with BBC Radio 1's Jo Whiley, 12 November 2002)

ORDINARY TALENT

How might one make the production of celebrity a little more predictable? The most recent answer is to attempt to generate celebrity from scratch. While celebrities themselves are increasingly exploring ways of controlling their own representations (Whannel, 2002: 184), some sections of the media production industries have found new and effective strategies for controlling the images *they* produce.

This is not a new idea of course. Historically, the first instincts of the media and entertainment industries have been towards vertical integration – taking control of the whole process of the production, distribution and sale of their products from start to finish. Consequently, the golden years of Hollywood are littered with stories of discovery, where the dental nurse or waitress is snapped up by the talent scout and offered a career in the movies, only to find themselves burned out and abandoned years later. Within such narratives, the star is the victim of a rapacious and careless industry in control of every aspect of their existence. The popular music industry, too, has its own stories which demonstrate that the industry has often valued its performers more for their market appeal than for their musical abilities. The rock'n'roll boom of the 1950s and early 1960s saw numerous young prospects being picked off the sidewalk for their brooding good looks only to reveal in the studio that they couldn't sing a note. Over their histories, the media and entertainment industries have routinely sought to find 'unspoiled' fresh prospects they could 'discover' and groom for stardom. The commercial purpose behind this, of course, is to take control of the individual's career from the beginning and to contract for their services into the future as a means of limiting the cost and maximising the returns to the original investor of the individual becoming a success. If, in some cases, these individuals turned out to have no particular talents, that was not necessarily a bad thing. What seems to have been more important was their determination to become 'somebody' and to do what was necessary to achieve this outcome. It is not hard to see how dealing with someone who was simply determined to be famous might have been easier than dealing with someone who had more subtle or specific goals and expressed preferences about the means taken to achieve them.

Since the late 1990s, however, there has been a spectacular revival of the media's interest in manufacturing celebrity. Some sections of the media, particularly commercial television, have discovered that rather than being merely the end-user of celebrity, they can produce it themselves. Increasingly, they have done this by using 'ordinary' people, with no special abilities and achievements, as the 'talent' in their programmes (Turner, 2010). Their celebrity is produced out of nothing, bypassing what we might think of as the conventional conditions of entry (specialised training, or a history of performance, for instance). Those who participate do not necessarily want to be singers, or actors, or dancers – they just want to be on television. These days it is clear that such a desire is actually quite widespread, as are the prospects for its satisfaction. Frances Bonner (2003) suggests that it is probably more common for people in the countries she examines (the UK and Australia) to have been on television, either as a participant or contestant or as a member of the live audience, than not. Her focus upon what she calls 'ordinary television' – game shows, infotainment, reality television, the less travelled formats for the television analyst but the quotidian mainstay of the television schedule – leads her to argue that television is omnivorous in its demand for 'ordinary people' to feature in its programming. According to Bonner's estimate, convincingly worked out in some detail, British television would feature close to one quarter of a million 'ordinary people' on screen per year, with over 20,000 having a speaking role (2003: 61–2).

Given the scale of the desire these figures reflect, it is not surprising that many television formats – in particular, reality-based gameshows, talent quests and docu-soaps – have oriented themselves towards satisfying it. In an exceptional number of cases, reality TV formats have been commercially successful. Internationally, *Big Brother* and *Idol* are among the most widely adopted examples of these formats but there is a wealth of reality TV formats that have attracted large audiences, both national and transnational, as well as creating their own stable of personalities and stars: *Survivor, Airport, Airline, Driving School, What Not to Wear, Jersey Shore, The Hills* and *Keeping Up With The Kardashians* are among them. For the media organisations involved – the producers and the network – the celebrity they manufacture for the contestants/subjects is not their primary objective: their goal is to develop a viable programming initiative to sell to advertisers. Celebrity is a profitable by-product, to be sure, but the producers have only a limited commitment to trading on it once the programme has gone to air. (For instance, the *Big Brother* producers must invest in successive waves of housemates, each replacing the last, in order to promote each series.) They know, however, celebrity's importance in attracting participants in the first place. For the subjects or contestants in reality TV programmes, even where substantial cash prizes or career opportunities are to be won, celebrity is the real prize that is on offer.

It is this phenomenon I want to discuss in the first part of this chapter. In reference to reality TV programmes such as *Big Brother*, I want to argue that these media producers have taken control of the economy of celebrity by turning it into an outcome of a programming strategy. Among the notable effects of this recasting of celebrity has been the producer's capture and containment of some of the core contradictions that structure the relation between the celebrity and the entertainment industries. Most crucially, they have contained the capacity (temporarily, at least) for damaging conflicts of interest to arise. Since the construction of celebrity is thoroughly incorporated into the programming format, any potentially conflicting personal and commercial objectives (that is, those of the celebrities-in-the-making, and those of the producers or networks) are structurally accommodated to each other from the beginning. As a result, these celebrities are especially dependent upon the programme that made them visible in the first place as they have virtually no other platform from which to address their audience.

Again, I realise this is not unprecedented and such patterns have occurred in the film industry at frequent points in its history. But the value and appeal of celebrity today seem to have radically empowered those media formats that produce it. It is understandable, therefore, if commentators express their concern about the long-term prospects of the temporary beneficiaries of this process. Although the 'ordinary person' can use *Big Brother* to take a shot at fame, something that was unlikely to be available to them through any other means, they are still at the mercy of the system that creates them and within which they have a very limited future. I don't think it is easy to be too categoric about this, however, and the examination of specific versions of *Big Brother* can generate quite different accounts of the power relations being played out. To run against the grain of the politics implied by that comment, then, in the second part of this chapter, I discuss what may appear to be an inversion of the politics of 'reality TV': the construction of a form of DIY celebrity, using personal websites, blogs and social media as a means of constructing fame and trading upon it. This development affects not only the ordinary person wishing to construct a public persona for themselves, but also increasingly the established celebrity wishing to change the means through which they negotiate the construction of their persona with their audience.

'REAL' CELEBRITIES AND REALITY TV

As we have seen, the discourses that construct celebrity are contradictory. According to them, celebrity is deserved or totally arbitrary: the recognition of natural talent or just blind good luck. Audiences place individual celebrities somewhere along a continuum that ranges from seeing them as objects of desire or emulation to regarding them as spectacular freaks worthy of derision. Mostly celebrities will attract one form of response rather than the other (so Sarah Jessica Parker might attract more admiration than, say, Jessica Simpson), but it is possible to attract both from different constituencies – or even from the same constituency. (By this I mean that the desire may incorporate an awareness of the cynicism behind the process of production; for instance, I could see Lady Gaga's followers occupying this sort of knowing but celebratory position.) This discursive contradiction is reflected in the paradoxical relationship between the celebrity and their public. Celebrity is the product of a commercial process but it is worth remembering that the public expression of popular interest can operate, at times, as if it was entirely independent of this commercial process. Sometimes no amount of publicity can generate public interest, while at other times the public will reveal a mind of its own in its reactions to a specific individual, no matter what the publicity machine does. There is a tension between these two forces – the commercial industry and the public will – and celebrity cannot be constructed or maintained without both playing some part. In the first part of this chapter, though, it is the arbitrariness – the constructedness – of celebrity that is most pertinent to the focus on its fabrication 'out of nothing'.

While television is the industry location I want to concentrate on here it is first worth noting the significance of the music industry's activities over the last decade or two, starting with the successful development of the Spice Girls. The Spice Girls seem to have been conceived, from the start, as a brand rather than a band. Developed by producers with very specific objectives in mind, they were the outcome of marketing plans rather than a grassroots fan or performance base. Nevertheless, in my view, it is possible to explain their level of success in comparison to other pre-fabricated bands of the time precisely because the individual members were able to construct convincing celebrity identities for themselves. Tempting though it is, now, to see them as the popular music industry's most elaborate expression of bad faith, I think a significant component of their appeal to their audiences was both their explicit acknowledgment of their commodification *and* their refusal to allow this to de-legitimise them. The 'cheekiness' that trade-marked their media presence was partly constituted by this combination of discourses of pragmatism and feisty independence, which allowed them to perform, convincingly, a knowing celebration of their own constructedness.

P. David Marshall (2000) makes a similar point in his discussion of The Beatles' success. According to him, The Beatles 'trod the line between something authentically wonderful and significant (*fab*ulous) and something manufactured and created by an industry (*fab*ricated)' (2000: 169). As Marshall had pointed out earlier, in *Celebrity and Power* (1997), the fundamental discursive opposition that structures achievement and celebrity in the music industry pits authenticity against in-authenticity. The 'true' rock star is the romantic artist, their music resisting the temptation to pander to commercial tastes in favour of expressing the self. As I have noted earlier, there is a commercial reason for emphasising the artistic integrity of the musician through discourses of authenticity, of course – it attaches fans to the artist, not just the latest single or music video, and thereby enhances the prospect of long-term careers (Weinstein, 1999). Despite this, and despite the continued currency of anti-commercial discourses that attack the ersatz, the 'sellout' and the demands of the record company, the music industry also has a long history of pre-fabricated bands. The Monkees are the most lurid historical example, possibly because it was widely reported that they did not play on their recording sessions and only one of them had any real credibility as a musician in his later career (Michael Nesmith), but there are plenty of other examples (Milli Vanilli, for instance).[1] With The Beatles, Lennon and McCartney's songwriting abilities and the credibility that came from learning their trade in the red-light districts of Hamburg provided the authenticity. The contrivance of their 'look' (the suits, the haircuts, the stage-managed press conferences, the Svengali-like presence of Brian Epstein) told us that they were being marketed as a product. Marshall argues that The Beatles are the place where we first encounter a distinctively modern take on fame. Their open manipulation of their public image might once have generated a negative connotation, but Marshall suggests instead that – in the case of The Beatles – the commodification of the musician was 'no longer seen as some form of corruption of artistic practice; rather it became *part* of the artistic process' (2000: 170).

Marshall also notices how the members of The Beatles actively sought to differentiate themselves as individuals. He describes their successful transition from being identified with the band to being identified as individual members of the band as a new form of authenticity, a 'democratic celebration of celebrity' (ibid.: 174). Something like this influenced the representation and self-presentation of the Spice Girls. It is possible to argue, although possibly difficult to remember when faced with their subsequent solo careers, that the Spice Girls, individually although in varied ways, gave the lie to the assumption that those who are exploited by the entertainment industries in this way are vacuous victims. Instead, they performed convincingly as examples of how savvy and tough-minded individuals can play the fame game, on the industry's terms, and still win. That, it seems to me, was the specific meaning of their championing of 'Girl Power'. 'Girl Power' was more convincing when performed as a collective manifesto, however; its impact, even its relevance, disappears when we look at the band members' careers as individuals after the band dissolved. In the long term, the Spice Girls' lesson for the industry was not about how to appropriate media power. Rather, it was a one-off demonstration of how we might successfully manufacture celebrity for consumption by a mass audience without attempting to disavow its inauthenticity.

None of the 'brand-bands' that followed the Spice Girls achieved an equivalent status – either in terms of the successful construction of individual identities for their members, or a cultural politics for the band, or in terms of commercial success. Nevertheless, there is some truth in Naomi Klein's (2000) observation that the pre-fab brand-band – typified at that time by N'Sync, All Saints and a whole raft of boy bands – has never been so prominent a phenomenon as it became at the end of the 1990s (although she may have been surprised by how long the boy band has survived – look at the current celebrity of One Direction, for instance). In addition, Klein suggests, 'musicians have never before competed so aggressively with consumer brands' by setting up their own line of merchandise. Sean 'Puffy' Combs, she goes on, 'has leveraged his celebrity as a rapper and record producer into a magazine, several restaurants, a clothing label and a line of foods' (2001: 50). One of the outcomes of this trend – the branding of pop bands – was its relocation to television in the early reality TV talent contest/ makeover hybrid, *Popstars*.

The *Popstars* format originated in New Zealand in 1999, before moving to Australia, and then to the UK and the USA over 2000–2001. The programme set out to construct a successful pop music group on television and the strategies it developed towards this end are now highly familiar. Hundreds of contestants were interviewed and their auditions filmed – and exploited – for a range of effects. Much of it was simply humiliating, with bad performances eliciting caustic 'private' conversations between the judges. Once the band members were chosen, the programme moved into a second phase as it followed the 'popstars' through their grooming and development right up to the release of their first recording. In each of the countries where I followed its course (New Zealand, Australia, the UK, and the USA), the popstars went on to form a band, release a single, and promote it successfully. While the initial success of some of these singles was extraordinary (the first UK and Australian singles, in particular, went to number one immediately), none of the bands were able to repeat that initial success or construct a continuing career. Typically, even those who remained together as a unit[2] found that they couldn't sustain sufficient audience interest in their music once they lost the public visibility generated by appearing weekly on prime-time television.

As that outline of the format will have suggested, *Popstars'* amalgam of television genres exerted quite an influence on the make-up of the formats which followed. The first phase of the format draws on the two competing paradigms of the TV talent quest (that is, those searching for genuine talent and those that set out to humiliate talentless contestants). Contestants are of both kinds (talented and talentless) and provide the pleasures of both formats in relatively equal proportions. (We can see such strategies still currently employed in various ways through contemporary formats such as *Got Talent, Idol,* and *The Voice.*) Since viewers are encouraged to follow the contest and try to pick the likely winners (in some versions they can vote for their preferred contestant), it also works like a game show. A docu-soap style narrative helps to structure this part of the contest, too, using interviews with family members and providing a certain amount of sentimental back-story for the higher profile contestants. The second phase mixes the makeover format with classic fly-on-the-wall reality television of the kind that would be more thoroughly developed by *Big Brother* (which first appeared in the Netherlands in 1999, with the UK version beginning in 2000), offering the appearance of the real and the everyday with the added attraction of being set backstage in a glamorous world that is the epitome of 'cool'. (Indeed, the programme spends much of its time teaching these contestants – and their audience – how to be 'cool'.) In its later iterations, the format has been applied to other industries or domains of celebrity – *Search for a Supermodel* is one example – and to the media's construction of celebrity itself, with *Fame Academy*.

Popstars offered the opportunity of fame and success within a narrow commercial framework: this is a prefab band, after all, so no matter how well you sing you had better not be fat or homely. Furthermore, the band already had its first single and album chosen for it: no room for 'musical differences' to arise here. Many professionals within the music industry regarded it as an extraordinarily cynical exercise that offended all the principles of artistic integrity and authenticity Marshall described as fundamental to the sector. And although it may well have been to some extent integrated into the economy of opportunity within the music industry, the contractual arrangements it negotiated with its performers were in at least some instances especially exploitative.[3] For the television networks, however, the show was an enormous ratings success. More importantly, it was a 'water cooler' success, generating lots of talk and media interest. It created considerable spin-off promotional opportunities such as shopping mall appearances and television specials, as well as concert performances. For particular sectors of the audience – teenage girls and young women – *Popstars* was must-see TV that vigorously fed into their everyday lives. (Notably, though, the novelty wore off with successive series.) For the celebrity industry, it demonstrated the value of saturation television exposure for short-term impact.

In *Popstars*, though, and for some of its imitators, there was still a connection between talent, winning the contest, and the ensuing celebrity (short-lived though the latter might be). Indeed, there are often indications that many of the contestants were already working in the industry concerned and using the programme as the chance for their 'big break'. *Big Brother*, still regarded as the ultimate pseudo-event, took us one step further away from this connection. Like *Popstars*, *Big Brother* is also an amalgam of a bunch of TV genres: the game-show, the lifestyle programme, the make-over, the talk show, and the reality TV docu-soap. As I am sure readers of this book will know, the format involves a cast of 'ordinary people' who agree to take up residence in a house or apartment for a set period during which every moment of their lives will be captured on camera. Each week, they nominate fellow 'housemates' for eviction so that the viewers may decide who stays and who leaves the house. The last housemate standing wins a cash prize. Since it is usually stripped across the week's schedule in repeated timeslots, each new series is major entertainment news. As a television event, it is big. To date it has been screened in more than 70 countries, and created spin-offs such as *Celebrity Big Brother* as well as many unofficial clones to date. Its aggregated audience would be numbered in the billions. In Italy the first series attracted 69 per cent of the national audience, and even in the US where it took a while to catch on (and the cast threatened to walk out!), it eventually picked up 52 per cent of the audience (Johnson-Woods, 2002: 1–2).[4] The scheduling details vary significantly across markets, so in some countries *Big Brother* is screened daily, in others three or four times a week. The regular episodes are often supplemented by highlights packages or in some markets an additional late night, 'uncut' or 'adult viewing' package (promising moments of nudity, swearing and sexual activity). In most cases there is a weekly eviction episode performed in front of a live audience. The website attached to the series has become an increasingly important component of the *Big Brother* event because of its interactivity: it has live camera feeds direct from the *Big Brother* location, chat rooms, blogs, social media links, picture galleries, highlights video, news and updates, gossip and merchandise, as well as facilities for on-line voting on evictions and so on. In the Australian version, the *Big Brother* house was in a theme park and the actual physical site has remained a continuing attraction outside the production cycles. Advertising is sold for the entire run of the series (in most cases several months, although the 'Celebrity' versions tend to be much shorter – a week in the UK for example) and is supported by lots of product placement. This varies from delivering Pizza Hut pizzas to the housemates for a treat, to simply providing the mop or the washing-up liquid.

The publicity and promotions potential of the format has proven to be extraordinary: the programme can be promoted as a news event, as a cultural phenomenon, as the launching pad for a raft of new celebrities, as a contest to be played through SMS and social media, and, finally, as high concept or special event television. As each housemate is evicted they generate a fresh news cycle: their eviction may be cited on channel and network news, they will be guests on talk and news magazine programmes, exploited through channel, network, or sponsors' promotions, and some may even turn up as presenters in new programming ventures. When each series is completed, the whole cast is processed through the various network programme formats all over again, with retrospectives, reunions, insider revelations and so on. Cross-promotion across television networks, websites, newspapers, magazines and radio is fundamental. Whenever it is scheduled, *Big Brother* generates a mini-boom in celebrity content because of this increase in material and interconnected promotional outlets, as well as its intrinsically controversial nature as a programming innovation. *Big Brother* creates its own celebrity and thus raises general interest in celebrities and their appeal, while also challenging us to consider why people would volunteer to participate – as well as why people want to watch. The news media have tended to deal with these two impulses in a disingenuous manner: they shamelessly exploit the celebrity gossip that *Big Brother* provides, while also soliciting comment pieces which warn about the programme's deleterious effect on 'television as we know it', or its worrying implications for our society.

Given such a production context, the *Big Brother* housemates are the epitome of the fabricated celebrity. While they are cast for their likely contribution to the overall performance and appeal of the programme, their casting does not reflect the possession of particular professional talents or abilities. Different countries have cast for different internal dynamics (in the USA they cast for conflict, in Australia they have tended to go for community, in Spain for sexuality), but most production companies have attempted to avoid to be seen preferring people whose ultimate aim is to be an entertainer of some kind.[5] These attempts have not been entirely successful, but the trend is for contestants to be 'ordinary' people without professional self-presentation skills or a theatrical or media background. If it were not for the fact that they have agreed to be on camera twenty-four hours a day, seven days a week for several months, they could plausibly stand in for the 'ordinary viewer'. The cash prize offered to the successful candidate is an attraction, but the real prize is the chance to be on television for months. Like those individuals Kylie Minogue refers to in this chapter's epigraph, these people want to be famous but most of them haven't worked out what for. *Big Brother* helps them to defer answering that question while making major steps towards achieving their objective.

Why do the contestants participate? For the most part, they are not looking for any special talents to be recognised: indeed, in many cases, they display none. The answer to this question is actually the obvious one: the contestants want to be on television long enough to be famous. *Big Brother* can almost guarantee that. Perhaps the more difficult question is why these people – having no special abilities to celebrate – should want to pursue fame at all. Braudy's discussion of fame is unusual (certainly for the period in which he wrote it), in that he dwells approvingly on the undeserved character of modern fame. Braudy regards the modern desire for fame as a perfectly reasonable impulse and explains some of its attractions. First, he points out that fame does more than offer us visibility; it offers a particularly flattering kind of visibility in which 'all blemishes are smoothed and all wounds healed'. Fame is the achievement of a magical moment of perfection, the end point of a process that restores 'integrity and wholeness' to the representation of the self. Second, and more importantly, to be famous in the arbitrary manner I am describing is especially validating for the individual: 'To be famous for yourself, for what you are without talent or premeditation, means you have come into your rightful inheritance'. Fame becomes a 'personal justification' (Braudy, 1986: 7).

The desire for such personal validation has a long history. Nick Couldry (2000a) refers to 'the fantasy of being included in some way in major cultural forms such as television or film' as being related to what 'Valerie

Walkerdine summarises in historical terms as the fantasy of "getting on the stage"' (2000a: 55). Popular culture has for many years provided a legitimate setting for that fantasy – from the boxing ring to the music hall and vaudeville to television – especially for members of the working class. Indeed, Couldry argues that among the attractions of this fantasy is its inferred capacity to free the individual from their class placement: specifically, they could escape their identification with the working class without defecting to the middle class. On the other hand, there is the argument that Skeggs and Wood (2012) make, which suggests that while the modes of personal comportment being recommended through such reality TV genres as makeover TV are clearly marked as middle class, the manner in which working-class audiences actually engage with these television texts reveals resistance to the imposition of these values, and even a defiant identification with precisely that mode of performance which does not conform to middle-class norms. There are resonances here with Andrew Ross's (1989) discussion of the function of popular culture which emphasised how many popular cultural forms deliberately provoked respectable society into distaste and condemnation. For the participants themselves, however, there is merit in Couldry's suggestion that the personal validation achieved through appearing on these programmes might provide an opportunity for sidestepping the normatising influence of class. Certainly, and while Bourdieu would have despised the kind of celebrity we are discussing here (imagine Bourdieu on Jade Goody, for instance), reality TV celebrity does seem to constitute a new variety of social distinction, gained without treading any of the conventional pathways. As a spectacular form of symbolic capital, reality TV celebrity opens up an almost instantaneous route to the achievement of a 'social life that will be known and recognised, which will free you from insignificance' (Bourdieu, 1990: 196.)

Couldry (2003) explores similar territory in his discussion of the performance of 'self-disclosure' through the media. He has quite a different take on celebrity here, however, in that he relates it to what he calls the 'myth of the media centre': the commonsense assumption that the media 'speak for' the centre of the social world. Access to the media therefore constitutes access to the social centre and is thus empowering in a more generally social sense than simply generating personal fame. Rather than an excess of narcissism, or an obsession with fame, Couldry describes the motivation behind the ordinary person's preparedness to expose themselves on television as the pursuit of personal access to a 'central' social space (2003: 116). As such, it is an essentially political enfranchisement that is the object. The participation he describes may be about utilising the symbolic power of the media rather than an investment in celebrity itself. This has been an extremely influential and useful idea, and it seems particularly persuasive in relation to the confessional talk show, the phenomenon Jane Shattuc deals with in *The Talking Cure* (1997) and Joshua Gamson in *Freaks Talk Back* (1998), but perhaps less so in relation to the participants of *Big Brother*.

Most of the early academic discussions of *Big Brother*, perhaps understandably then, do not focus on such issues but instead concentrate first on reality TV's place in the history of television's construction of 'the real' (Roscoe, 2001, for instance, or more substantially, Hill, 2002, and 2007). Jon Dovey (2000) contextualises the historical shift in the relation between the television camera and the real in this way. Once the camera was hidden and determined not to interfere with the reality it depicted, implying the priority of the pro-filmic events, of 'the real' over the representation. Now, however, the camera captures events 'that are *only* happening because the camera is there', implying the priority of the representation over 'the real'. In reality TV, in particular, from make-over programmes to *Popstars*, says Dovey, 'the entire process is only happening because it is going to be on television'; that is, a 'reality' is constructed solely in order to produce a representation. For all concerned, this is the blindingly obvious but nonetheless crucial and often overlooked implication, that 'without the fame-conferring gaze, there would be no event worth filming, no reality' (2000: 11).

Implicit here is the growing importance of the camera as a means of constituting and validating everyday reality. Just as the fans at a sports event cheer when they see their images come up on the big screens in the stadium, celebrating their media presence, the circulation of images of the self via television has become a means of legitimation. No longer consigned to the 'hyperreal' of postmodernity, the media-tised image of the self has come to seem as if it is among the promises of everyday existence. According to Frances Bonner's (2003) argument mentioned earlier, this is becoming an increasingly plausible expectation for sections of the community. Inside the idea of reality TV is the offer to display our everyday identities as a spectacle, as an experiment, as entertainment – and television's insatiable appetite for ordinary people to display their identities ensures that the offer is made to an increasing number of prospective participants. On the other hand, of course, the offer is made in a highly selective manner; the contestants for *Big Brother* are chosen from many thousands of applications and we do not know the criteria that determined the selection process. Nonetheless, the term 'reality TV' sets out to eliminate the distance between television and everyday existence, and the distance does seem to be shrinking. To the many who participate in these programmes, who turn up in the audiences of live programmes, and who race home to see if they made it onto the television coverage of their favourite sporting event, everyday life is at its most valid and real when it is visible on TV.

With *Big Brother*, the celebrities in the making are explicitly disconnected from discourses of the exceptional by the programme's format. What audiences see is the housemates' 'everyday' behaviour, nothing more or less. Of course, it is important to acknowledge that this was in itself a performance (Roscoe, 2001); we still may not know how these people behave every day when there are no cameras around. Nevertheless, among the attractions of the programme was precisely this promise of witnessing 'the everyday'. Even the voyeuristic attractions of watching the housemates shower or have sex – highly important to the promotion of the programme in most markets but not particularly important to the viewers' experience in the end (see Hill, 2002) – are articulated to a narrative that has us observing these people living their lives rather than performing a role. The magical discourses that surround conventional celebrities operate as teasing provocations to the demand for the revelation of the private. With *Big Brother* the reverse is true: private revelations are offered as the opening move in a process that turns these people into celebrities.

On the evidence of *Big Brother*'s consumption, this offer seems to have been widely accepted, and audiences entered into a direct process of narrative investment and identification. Such a process does not necessarily indicate sympathy or that their identification was positive. There are plenty of reasons to believe many viewers watched *Big Brother* from positions that explicitly 'dis-identified' with these people (the comments on the websites and social media would certainly indicate this). Many newspaper commentators also recorded their failure to 'get it' – to understand the appeal of the programme. Further, there seems to be an almost anthropological dimension to the programme's consumption by some sectors of the audience. In Australia, where the housemates were overwhelmingly drawn from the young, a steady growth in the over-55s audience suggests that this was an opportunity to observe a cultural fraction that was something of a mystery to this section of the audience. Little wonder that reality TV's complicated relation to the real has so dominated academic accounts.

The discourses of possibility that fuel the production and consumption of celebrity generally seem to have been thoroughly cashed in through this television format. If celebrity is increasingly possible as a career option; if its achievement is increasingly recognised as a matter of luck; and if television's role in making celebrities visible to us has become a major part of its programming strategies (i.e., through all kinds of programming from news to *Entertainment Tonight* to *Biography* to *Who Do You Think You Are?*); then it is perhaps not surprising that there are many people in the television audience who want to take the option provided by *Big Brother*. If the ideologies that inform celebrity in contemporary culture – the ideologies described by

P. David Marshall as entirely complicit with democratic capitalism – are fulfilling their function, the pursuit of celebrity as an objective rather than as a by-product of personal activity is not surprising either. Public visibility *per se* is offered as an achievement to emulate and desire; little wonder that it is pursued with such tenacity and at some personal risk by a large number of people. What *Big Brother* offers is precisely what such a desire creates: the promise of media validation for just being who you are, every day.

TAKING CONTROL: DIY CELEBRITY IN THE DIGITAL ERA

'Why are they doing this, do you think?' Coleridge asked. 'Why do you think? To get famous'. 'Ah, yes, of course,' said Coleridge. 'Fame'. 'Fame', he thought, 'the holy grail of a secular age'. The cruel and demanding deity that had replaced God. The one thing. The only thing, it seemed to Coleridge, that mattered any more. The great obsession, the all-encompassing national focus, which occupied 90 per cent of every newspaper and 100 per cent of every magazine. Not faith, but fame. 'Fame', he murmured once more. 'I hope they enjoy it'. 'They won't', Geraldine replied. (Ben Elton, *Dead Famous*, 2001: 242–3)

In 1996, among the more notorious sites accessible through the internet was Washington DC web designer Jennifer Ringley's 'JenniCam' site, which uploaded new photos of Jenni's bedroom every few minutes. The occasional flashes of nudity helped to attract media attention to her site, and Jenni became something of a celebrity (she eventually appeared as a guest star in the TV series *Diagnosis Murder* – playing a webcam star). In the first edition of this book, which was published in 2004, I spent some time discussing the phenomenon of the many 'cam-girls' who appeared in JenniCam's wake. At that time, these sites featured live or recorded images of the cam-girl host, as well as other material such as comments, poetry, diaries, journals and so on. The cam-girls competed against each other to attract subscribers and fans, and a lively critical subculture built up where the cam-girls and their fans discussed the various tactics employed. Discourses of authenticity, commercialisation, and exploitation – all familiar from other areas of popular culture that are more thoroughly in the capture of commercial industries – framed the debates within this critical culture about what was acceptable behaviour from a cam-girl wishing to attract visitors to her site.

At the time, the cam-girls seemed an extremely clear example of web-based DIY celebrity, both in terms of the potential on offer and the dangers to the individual that came with this potential (their proximity to pornography sites, for instance, was one of the concerns) (Couldry, 2003: 129).

Most notably, this form of celebrity had been established in ways that were, largely, structurally independent of the mainstream media. In comparison to their counterparts in television or popular music, the cam-girls' integration into the mainstream media industries was initially minimal: they created their own sites, they generated their own content, and they designed their own performances of themselves. Surviving outside the industrial structure that produces the television personality or the film star, this was the cyberspace equivalent of a cottage industry. It was enabled by the growth of the personal website as a form of personal expression as well as a means of public self-presentation. For many observers (for example, Cheung, 2000: 47), the personal website as it existed in the late 1990s was an emancipatory medium, liberating the ordinary person from their constrained role as merely the consumer of media products[6]. Hence, there was significant interest in this particular use of the capacities of the online environment at the time.

Today, however, as cam-girl ethnographer Theresa Senft was told by one informant, 'cam girls are *so* 1998' (2008: 11). If we want to examine the potential for DIY celebrity online today, we need to look somewhere else. The passing of the cam-girls had three primary causes: 'the cultural saturation of webcams beyond early adopters', the 'rapid rise of broadband penetration around the world', and the rise of 'social networking services that now easily support text, still images, audio and video' (Senft, ibid.). Simply, the capacities exploited by the cam-girls became more widely available, and the widespread take-up of networked social media made much of what they did so routine as to be unremarkable. (Once you have a camera in every laptop, tablet and mobile phone, the webcam starts to lose its novelty!) Consequently, the opportunities for all kinds of DIY celebrity multiplied and diversified – creating what Senft describes as 'micro-celebrity': a 'new style of online performance that involves people in "amping up" their popularity over the Web using technologies like video, blogs, and social networking sites' (ibid.: 25). In this section of the chapter, then, I want to consider this next model of DIY celebrity, where certain techniques for celebrity production have been appropriated by members of the public, before turning to an examination of how similar capacities are enabling the more traditional media celebrity to gain new kinds of control over the presentation and circulation of their own public persona.

This is territory, I should add, that significantly blurs the distinction between production and consumption which organises this book, and is all the more interesting for that. Indeed, what the micro-celebrity demonstrates, as James Bennett notes, is the fact that not only has the desire to be famous become 'increasingly ordinary', but so have many of 'the tools with which to become famous' (2011: 179) – the techniques used to publicise the self through personal websites, blogs, and social media such as Facebook, MySpace and Twitter. The micro-celebrity engages in a form of self-branding that is prosecuted through the presentation of their persona online: 'micro-celebrity involves viewing friends or followers as a fan base; acknowledging popularity as a goal; managing the fan base by using a variety of affiliative techniques; and constructing an image of self than can be easily consumed by others' (Marwick and boyd, 2011: 141). P. David Marshall argues that this development complicates the production/consumption division in a particular way: rather than merely thinking of celebrity as the product of representation, Marshall describes social media as forms of 'presentational media' where we encounter an expression of the self that differs from those enabled by previous media platforms because it is not 'entirely interpersonal in nature nor is it entirely highly mediated or representational' (2010: 35). This, he suggests, takes us into new territory for studies of the media: it constitutes the partial displacement of a representational media system with what he calls a 'presentational culture' (ibid.: 45) in which the individual not only sees the public presentation of the self as a productive mode of self-fashioning, but also grasps the opportunity of taking personal control of that process.

Typically, the micro-celebrity operates within a relatively limited and localised virtual space, drawing on small numbers of fans such as the followers of a particular subcultural practice. Some, such as the celebrity blogger Perez Hilton, have parlayed their modest DIY beginnings into a major online presence that is of equivalent scale and structure to that of more traditional media celebrities. Such a career trajectory actually ends up compromising any claim one might want to make about ordinary people's capacity to generate an alternative form of celebrity through these strategies; the more their small-scale DIY presence expands, and the more followers it attracts, the more it comes to resemble those conventional forms of fame to which it may once have claimed to provide an alternative (Bennett, 2011: 181).

Nonetheless, the accessibility of the means of publicity and distribution now available online does at least offer the possibility that ordinary people need no longer deal with the traditional media gatekeepers before they are able to attract public attention. Not only does this facilitate the small-scale activities of the micro-celebrities, but it has also laid new pathways to the acquisition of mainstream fame. As a result, the traditional media and cultural intermediaries we discussed in Chapter 2 no longer totally control all the possibilities: there are now some entry points over which both the prospective celebrity and their audience have some control. The music industry, for instance, generates many examples of artists and bands whose careers were launched through exposure on MySpace (Lilly Allen and the Arctic Monkeys are the usual ones mentioned here), and there is the example of teenage star Justin Bieber, whose career began as a result of the viral success of a video his mum posted on YouTube (Rojek, 2012: 33). Of course, hoping to go viral on YouTube may be just as arbitrary a process for acquiring fame as any that have preceded it, but the power relations are now slightly different: significantly, the role of the consumer has been strengthened. That is, Marwick and boyd have argued, the public's capacity to 'exercise control' over the process of celebritisation has increased (2011: 155).

This, however, takes us into the second area I wanted to explore here – the way in which the techniques of the micro-celebrity, themselves borrowed from the publicity and promotions industries, have in turn been 'borrowed back' by the 'real' celebrities – those who operate within mainstream commercial media structures – in order to increase *their* control over their own celebritisation. Given the comprehensiveness with which the media's management of celebrity controls the construction of a particular celebrity's presentation of their persona and their relation with their audience, it is not surprising that it is now common for celebrities to use social media, and particularly Twitter, not only as a means of communicating with their fans, but also in order to regain some personal control over their relationship with their public. Making use of social media in this way has become essential for anyone working in the media and entertainment industries these days. For some, such as Tom Cruise, the use of a Twitter feed is a relatively seamless extension of an already existing official publicity strategy: he has acknowledged he does not write his own tweets, for instance. As used by others, however, such as Mariah Carey or Ashton Kutcher, Twitter offers something new: a mode of direct, apparently unmediated, access to their fans. Kutcher, in particular, seems to regard Twitter as something of a personal media playground and appears unconcerned about surrendering his privacy, or that of his former wife, Demi Moore (his 2009 posting of a photo of Moore bending over in a white bikini became notorious). As a result, the pre-eminent objective of the fan – to find out what the celebrity is 'really' like – appears to be more categorically achieved through their engagement via Twitter rather than any other platform. Celebrities read and respond to tweets from their fans – sometimes directly, and sometimes simply by re-tweeting. They also converse with each other – celebrity to celebrity—and allow their followers to eavesdrop on that conversation. Of course, the belief that we are reading an authentic comment actually uttered by our favourite celebrity may still be illusory; it may still be written by an employee. That there is no way of knowing this for sure appears to be no disincentive for the followers. Indeed, evaluating the message for its authenticity and provenance seems to simply add interest to the game of interpreting the performance of celebrity in play. Not only is this about authorship, but also, as Marwick and boyd note, 'it is the inability to tell what is strategic and what is accidental, as well as what is truthful and what is not, that makes Twitter so enjoyable for fans' (2011: 153). Hence the exorbitant numbers of followers collected by some of the more high profile tweeters; these figures will date as soon as I write them, but they give some idea of the scale we are talking about: Lady Gaga has 15 million followers on Twitter and Justin Bieber has 14 million. It is said that the tweets sent by popular British media figure, Stephen Fry, are read by more people than all the 'printed copies of *The Times, The Telegraph, The Financial Times, The Guardian* and *The Independent* combined' (van Krieken, 2012: 134).

The scale of this potential market is one of the reasons why, at the moment, a professional engagement with Twitter is fundamental for virtually anyone interested in managing their public persona. Politicians tweet relentlessly, using the implied directness and authenticity of this communication channel as, among other things, a means of counteracting common conceptions of the politician as remote, inaccessible, and out of touch with the ordinary person; this, in addition to touting policy initiatives and positions. We have also seen the enhanced celebritisation of journalists[7] through their participation on Twitter. This is not necessarily only in order to prosecute their own personal brand, however. Twitter has become core business as most news organisations now require their journalists to maintain a Twitter account as a means of attracting readers, listeners or viewers to their news services. For their part, journalists are finding Twitter a valuable news source, as well as a means of building a public profile for a professional persona that is in some respects independent of their employer. The Twitter-led celebritisation of the journalist constitutes the conclusion of a long-term trend towards the personalisation of news: this trend has taken us from a world in which news stories were more credible without a byline (thus signifying their total objectivity), to a world in which the journalist has become part of the advertising pitch, as well as a form of authorisation, for the story.

Not only does the celebrity use social media to take personal control of their public presentation in the way these examples suggest, but they also use them to take advantage of unmediated communication with their fans. The intention behind this latter objective may be just as strategic as any other mode of image management, of course: some celebrities clearly see Twitter as offering them their own dedicated media channel, through which they can shape what the rest of the media say about them, as well as determining what their fans – most importantly – believe about them. Anthea Taylor

(2013) has discussed 'celebrity feminist' Naomi Wolf's deployment of Twitter as a means of shaping the reception of her most recent, and poorly reviewed, book, *Vagina*. Taylor shows how Wolf has used Twitter to disseminate the positive accounts of her book, while blanking out the negatives, retweeting only the positive feedback she receives (including from other celebrity admirers such as Courtney Love).

Another dimension to this is that, for some celebrities, Twitter seems to offer an opportunity to bypass even their own agents and public relations staff, breaking free of corporate image-management in order to gain the reward of direct communication with their fans, as well as some useful street-cred as a celebrity who has 'bucked the system' and undermined the publicity process by speaking honestly and directly to their fans. A risky tactic, because it implicitly demands that at least some of the content of the tweets should run against the grain of the more corporatised and established persona, and therefore may undermine the legitimacy of that persona. Of course, there would be little point in doing this at all if there was nothing at least slightly surprising about these messages. As a result, there are plenty of instances of tweets or comments on Facebook pages which have embarrassed those charged with managing the celebrity-commodity's fragile public persona – even though, at the same time, they may well have added an interesting new dimension to the celebrity's relationship with their fans. Nonetheless, in celebrity news today, one of the most commonly cited signs of a celebrity caving in to stress or exhibiting signs of mental disturbance is the posting or tweeting of inappropriate or unusually candid comments about their private lives. A recent example of this was the media coverage of Whitney Houston's death.

Such activity inevitably reduces the distance between the celebrity and their audience. In an extremely useful article on celebrity practice and Twitter, upon which I have drawn repeatedly in this section, Marwick and boyd contend that socially networked media has fundamentally changed celebrity culture:

> Gossip websites, fan sites and blogs provide a plethora of new locations for the circulation and creation of celebrity, moving between user-generated content and the mainstream media. The fragmented media landscape has created a shift in traditional understanding of 'celebrity management' from a highly controlled and regulated institutional model to one in which performers and personalities actively address and interact with fans. (2011: 140)

They go on to describe the consequent change as 'structural', in that 'it complicates the locations of power, the avenues of access, and the management of the celebrity-commodity' by the media industries (ibid.: 142).

The aspect that is most affected by these new developments, of course, is the nature of the para-social relation between the fan and the celebrity. Communicating via Twitter or Facebook, fans now can actually engage in a visible and public exchange with their favourite celebrity; they can receive responses to their questions or comments. Fans can also attract some celebrity to themselves with repeated interactions over time. Through this expanded domain of interactivity, there are now substantial elements of this para-social relationship which no longer look like the simulation of a conventionally social relationship at all. This is far from being a categoric shift, of course, and much of the interactivity we have been describing could indeed be regarded as simply the relocation of traditional strategies of marketing and publicity onto another platform of distribution. This is why Marwick and boyd are right to describe the current situation in terms of how 'complicated' the structure of relations has now become. However, it does seem that the capacities for direct interaction that social media generate between the fans and the celebrity are marked by enhanced levels of familiarity, disclosure, responsiveness, and possibly even of sincerity (Marwick and boyd, 2011: 149).

That said, however, Marwick and boyd are quick to point out that while Twitter does to some extent bring famous people and fans "closer" together, … it does not equalize their status' (ibid.: 155); as indeed the fans seem to acknowledge through the manner of their interaction, the power differentials may have shifted, but they have not gone away. Rojek puts it this way:

> The essence of the star is to be out of the reach of ordinary people … For all the inside dope, the tales of chance meetings, the bits and bobs from Web chat rooms that afford fans the secrets and low-down on celebrity culture, the balance of power in information and opinion shaping is overwhelmingly in the hands of the celebrity and the adjoining PR-Media hub. (2001:124)

It is easy to overstate the significance and extent of the increasing power of the consumer/fan, and so it is worth noting how little the overarching patterns of economic, cultural and political power have changed – notwithstanding the possibility that the changes we are witnessing now are indeed structural. Similarly, for those who take up the challenge of constructing their own DIY celebrity online; they are reminded that 'practising celebrity' and 'having celebrity status are different' (Marwick and boyd, 2011: 156). This raises questions about the issue of scale, about whether we need to make very different arguments about the function of a niche presence in a fragmented mediascape than those we would make about a more traditionally mass-mediated presence. I think that there is a genuine question about whether the online celebrity we have talked about as a micro-celebrity is in fact the same, in most important respects, as a mass media celebrity.

This is another area of contemporary media experience where improved access or improved consumer choice has been equated with a process of democratisation, even in relation to such an apparently hierarchical context as the production of celebrity. Notwithstanding a growing body of evidence which challenges such an equation (Hindman, 2009; Turner, 2010), the link so often made between the affordances of new media and the proposal of an intrinsically democratising empowerment is still around, and it is that issue we will address in the following chapter.

NOTES

1 The Monkees were made for television, though, not the music industry. Television was also the medium for another early, but more honest, example of the fabrication of the star. Scottish singer, Sheena Easton, was the subject of a British television documentary that set out to examine if it was possible to manufacture a successful pop star and which ended by launching her on an unexpectedly lengthy career.
2 In the first Australian programme, one of the successful contestants dropped out almost immediately after she was chosen – well before the conclusion of the programme. The producers encouraged the media to canvass rumours that she had stolen from one of her colleagues, but other industry rumours suggested that she was not prepared to sign a contract that would have greatly restricted her earning capacity and autonomy for a number of years.
3 In the Australian example, members of the first *Popstars* band, Bardot, have lent tacit assent to a report that the percentage of their total earnings, which went to the television production company, Screentime, could have been as high as 60 per cent.
4 Toni Johnson-Woods goes through some of the early variations of format around the world (length, voting procedures and so on) in her *Big Bother* (2002). A full list of the series in the various countries to date, as well as access to the official websites is accessible through the Endemol *Big Brother* website at www.big-brother.nl.
5 There are some variations on this. In the UK and Australia, producers were keen to play down any previous media experience their housemates might have had in order to emphasise their ordinariness and thus to make more spectacular their eventual transition to media celebrities. However, in some European versions, in France for instance, there was a deliberate attempt to cast people with experience in the sex industries – dancers, strippers, even prostitutes – in order to ensure a higher likelihood of on-screen sexual activities.
6 There is a similar take on the phenomenon, as 'domestic webcams', in an interesting piece by Andreas Kitzmann from around the same period, 1999.
7 I am indebted to Anthea Taylor for drawing my attention to this point.

4 Celebrity, the Tabloid and the Democratic Public Sphere

INTRODUCTION

The influence of celebrity, while pervasive right across the media, has been especially pronounced on certain kinds of media product. In television, for example, it has become an increasingly significant component of news and current affairs programming. It has also been fundamental to the format of successful network talk shows such as *Oprah*, *Parkinson* and *Graham Norton*, and an increasingly important objective for guests appearing on confessional talk shows such as *Jerry Springer*, *Trisha* and *Ricki Lake* as well as reality TV game-show hybrids like *Big Brother*. The internet is littered with celebrity pictorial and video sites, ranging from the official and the anodyne to the mischievous and scandalous. In the print media, celebrity journalism has completely dominated the tabloid newspaper market in the UK, as well as the 'supermarket tabloids' such as the *National Enquirer* and the *Globe* in the USA, and it has created the genre of the celebrity weekly magazine. Celebrity content has been fundamental to the reinvention of the mass market women's magazine. In the United States, the UK, Europe, Australia and Canada (at least), since the late 1980s, such magazines have revised their editorial mixes in response to falling circulations and competition from the new local celebrity weeklies and international glossy monthlies. While still retaining their traditional interest in fashion, domestic advice and 'beauty', the mass market women's magazines have progressively increased their focus on 'celebrity culture' (Gough-Yates, 2003: 136).

Cultural and media studies accounts of these developments have attempted to interpret the social and political implications of the increasing interest in celebrity. While the spectrum of views is wide, it tends to be organised around what is a significant division of opinion. On the one hand there are those who regard this trend as a lamentable example of the dumbing-down of the public sphere, as 'proper' news is replaced by gossip (see Langer, 1998). This is particularly prevalent among those who are interested in defending what they regard as more serious journalism (e.g., Franklin, 1997). On the other hand, there are those who welcome the mass media's emancipation from their obsession with the public, the institutional and the masculine (see Hartley, 1999; Lumby, 1997). Those who take this latter view regard what is now routinely described as the 'tabloidisation' of the public sphere as providing an opportunity for some democratisation of media access; as new, hitherto marginalised and often usefully undisciplined voices – those of the 'people formerly known as the audience' (Rosen, 2006) – are now being heard. In this chapter, I first want to review the establishment of celebrity in the area most conventionally regarded as both the beachhead (that is, the first point of 'invasion') and the heartland of this form of media content: mass market magazines. I will then address the broader 'tabloidisation' debate – the arguments between those who perceive a democratic potential in current media developments and those who don't – before looking at the application of this debate to the production of celebrity.

CELEBRITY, MASS MARKET MAGAZINES AND THE TABLOIDS

The key provocation for the late 1980s to early 1990s change in the content of the mass market women's magazines, according to Anna Gough-Yates' (2003) account of the British market, was competition from the celebrity weeklies. In many other markets the threat may not have been quite as direct, but the outcomes were similar as even the market leaders revised their editorial mix towards a much greater proportion of celebrity stories. In Holland, in fact, the trend had begun much earlier, with the 'gossip magazine' developing into a distinct genre incorporating practical advice and horoscopes alongside articles about celebrities, television stars and royalty during the 1970s (Hermes, 1995: 119). There and elsewhere, while the traditional components of the mass market women's magazine may have remained in place – the beauty hints, the fashion, the horoscopes, the advice columns and so on – they lost their prominence among the screamers on the front cover to the latest gossip from national television and Hollywood. Increasingly, also, the mass market women's magazines took on the need to represent their own cultural identities in a more aggressive and coherent fashion; an attempt to construct 'the personality' of the magazine in relation to the projected identities of their readers (Gough-Yates, 2003: 20). Such a strategy certainly enabled the women's magazines to modernise and survive: in Australia, it took them to new heights of circulation for almost a decade. It also played a part in the modernisation of mass market magazines for young girls over this period: the leading teen magazines in the UK and Australia, *Sugar* (which was reduced to a website in 2011) and *Dolly* (which still publishes), for example, were thoroughly dependent upon celebrity content. However, the incorporation of such a strategy into these sectors of the magazine market could not hold off the development of what became a new genre of mass-market magazine, the celebrity gossip and news weekly.

Since the 1990s, then, there has been a whole segment of the market devoted to these magazines, and while much of their content is in fact local (national sports or television stars, for instance, or Euro-trash royals for *Hello!* and its parent, *Hola!*) they have a major international presence as well. *Hello!* and *OK!* are ubiquitous in news outlets around the western world as are the more downmarket US variants such as *Us* and *The National Enquirer*. In large markets such as the UK and the USA there is quite a spectrum available. At the bottom end of the market, we have sleazy pictorial magazines that come and go, bearing names like *Celebrity Flesh*; their content is primarily nude or topless pictures sourced from newspaper paparazzi shots from around the world, or through production or video capture stills from screen performances. This sector is in some decline now, as competition from digital media pushes them aside, and as much of their content has been captured by tabloid dailies such as *The Sun* in the UK. Slightly above them in the market (but much more stable commercially) are the shock and sensation weeklies such as *The Star* or *The National Enquirer* which publish news stories and gossip as well as images of celebrities. Similar to these, but slightly less scandalous in their news values, are the gossip news weeklies such as *Who* (Australia), *People* (the USA) or *Now* (the UK); in these magazines, the stories come with an occasional coating of scepticism and the photos can be used to set celebrities up as objects of ridicule as well as admiration. At this lower end of the market (and as we saw in Chapter 2), the magazine's commercial alignment with the interests of the publicity industries varies considerably. A weekly such as *The National Enquirer* has only a limited dependence on celebrity gossip, but the gossip it does print tends to be scandalous, salacious and potentially damaging for its subjects. By no means does all of its news involve celebrities, however, and at various times it will deal with (and, as the O.J. Simpson case revealed, sometimes even break) major news stories. Most crucially, though, it (perhaps surprisingly) prides itself on its accuracy and this clearly limits the extent to which it could ever be fully incorporated into the publicity agenda of the major agencies (see Bird, 2002). With *Now*, however, and the American version of *People*, despite their enthusiastic contribution to the trade in paparazzi images and constant excitement over minor celebrity scandals, there is some commercial alignment between their news items and the promotional needs of the major entertainment industry organisations.

These industrial links are even more evident in the central sector of the crowded UK celebrity magazine market where the market leaders *OK*, *Heat* and *Hello!* (among many others) woo their readers by offering positive pictures and gossip features about celebrities. While *The National Enquirer* may not care to enter into ongoing relationships with the publicity industry, *Hello!* and *OK* certainly do. These magazines deal with almost nothing but celebrity[1] and thus they must be tightly articulated to the industry and its promotional needs if they want a reliable supply of pictures and stories. As a result, *Hello!* publishes uniformly appreciative features about celebrities' new marriages/ houses/babies, their recoveries from tragedy/divorce/career setbacks – clearly in collaboration with the celebrities concerned. *OK* is slightly less respectful of the celebrities it promotes, adopting a more populist and cheeky tone in its journalism, but nonetheless the magazine presents an overwhelmingly friendly view of the celebrities' lives to the reader. Both are highly respectable magazines. (*Hello!* is particularly so, going for glamour rather than sex, giving any whiff of scandal a fairly wide berth, and peppering its pages with respectful coverage of the activities of obscure Euro-royals.) Both share a curiously parochial and middle-class perspective (Conboy, 2002: 149), and despite their international circulation they are a world away from the chic cosmopolitanism of American glossies such as *Vanity Fair*.

The key competitor for these in the UK market is the slightly trashier, or at any rate slightly less respectable, *Heat*. *Heat* is cheekier, less sophisticated and more news-oriented (that is, it publishes more gossip) rather than feature-oriented (that is, staged promotions). It does not go in for the classic *Hello!* multi-page photo-spread on the celebrity at home – and so it does not carry so many of the signs of a commercial collaboration with the celebrity industry – but its treatment of the celebrity is still very positive and sympathetic. The cover price is lower and its target market younger and less middle class:[2] with a contemporary music-mag look, it has more street credibility for this demographic than either competitor. At one point, *OK* tried to steal *Heat*'s market by launching a spoiler campaign which involved a *Heat* look-alike (called *Hot Stars*) as a give-away with each issue of *OK*; *Hot Stars* shamelessly mimicked *Heat*'s layout, format and overall look.

A further dimension to this market, although not something that is usually noticed, is the manner in which celebrity content – gossip, pictures and so on – has infiltrated the online presence of news outlets that would otherwise see themselves as the locations of 'quality' rather than tabloid journalism. Although the print versions of newspapers such as *The Guardian* may carry little of this kind of content, the online version carries much more – and in more prominent positions. As I write, the home page of today's edition of *The Guardian* (18 January 2013) features stories on

William H. Macy, Lindsay Lohan, Megan Fox, Jamie Foxx, indie sister act Sara, and much more. This pattern can be seen in the quality press in other locations as well: the Fairfax newspapers in Australia, for instance, the most respected part of the quality press there, give far greater prominence to celebrity news online than in their print versions. This is a sufficiently widespread strategy to suggest that it is being vigorously employed by the high end of the newspaper market to compete with the more tabloid print outlets, as well as with online celebrity news sites, by addressing what are perceived to be the preferred interests of those who will look online first for their news and gossip.

To complete the spectrum I have been sketching out, there are probably two more layers. First, is the international movie/television magazine typified by *Premiere*, which exists solely to promote the industry's latest productions, with interviews, reviews, previews and so on. Given their relation to the industry, this is not the place to find the cheeky, the sceptical, or anything that might threaten the commercial success of the projects it promotes. In terms of circulation it has to be said that this is not a large sector of the market, and could be classified as belonging to the 'special interests' section of the magazine market. Second, and more commercially important, is what I would regard as the final layer: the top end of the market – the international (or probably more accurately, the 'glocal'[3]) quality glossy, ranging from, say, *FHM* to *Cosmopolitan* or *Vanity Fair*. While these magazines may observe more independent editorial policies than the movie magazines, it is important to note how thoroughly the transnational entertainment and media industries coordinate their interests with those of the high quality international glossies. We have already referred to Toby Young's (2001) account of his experience of working for *Vanity Fair* in New York, where he expressed alarm at how much power the entertainment industry agents and publicists enjoyed in determining what would be published about their clients in the magazine. His experiences would seem indicative of the broader relationship between such magazines and the celebrity industry. In fact, it would seem that the commercialisation of this relationship is deepening. Upmarket international magazines dealing with fashion, consumption, the arts, style, and other popular cultural topics (such as *Vanity Fair*, *Harper's Bazaar* and *Vogue*) have accorded celebrity news and features an ever more prominent position in their editorial mix. Stories on Sarah Jessica Parker or Jennifer Lopez are as likely to appear at this end of the market as they are to turn up in *Heat* or *People* – and they will likely be almost as anodyne and commercially helpful there as they would be in *OK*. It is important to emphasise this fact because criticisms of the effect of the promotion of celebrities upon the contemporary practice of journalism often assume that this is at its most active at the 'tabloid' end of the print media. My research on mass market magazines would suggest the reverse – that the alignment of the commercial interests of the magazine and the celebrity is at its most seamless at the higher end of the market.

Nevertheless, to assume that it is all the tabloids' fault would be an understandable error to make in the circumstances. This is especially the case in the UK, where the tabloid newspapers (the so-called 'red-tops') long ago hitched their wagon to the popular appetite for celebrity stories (Bromley and Cushion, 2002). Certainly, the British tabloids have almost categorically redefined what qualifies for them as news, so that tabloid news is now utterly personalised and dominated by reports on the actions of well-known people – politicians, public officials, sportsmen and women, celebrities, soon-to-be celebrities and wannabe celebrities. While broadsheets such as *The Observer* largely devote their weekend colour supplements to news background and lifestyle features, *The Mirror* and *The Express* devote their weekend colour supplements entirely to celebrities. Celebrity gossip achieves front-page status regularly and the whole sector has been influenced by *The News of the World*'s dogged pioneering of what has been called 'bonk journalism' (that is, 'who's doing it with whom'). This mode of journalism is deliberately salacious and careless of its effect on the persons concerned. Celebrities are fair game. The industry's incorporation of such an irresponsible attitude has been progressively uncovered by the phone-hacking scandal that began in 2005 and has continued until the present; this has revealed widespread abuse of the media's power as tabloid journalists hacked into the mobile phones of celebrities, members of the royal family and other newsworthy persons for material. The allegation that such practices had become routine, and were not only tolerated but also encouraged by management, resulted in the abrupt closure of *The News of the World* in 2011 and a major review of the regulation of the British press in 2012, and it may yet lead to changes in the regulatory environment in the UK in the future.

Even without the provocation of this particular episode, the tabloid press, particularly in the UK, has long had a highly fraught relationship with the celebrity industry. From an ethical point of view, it would be hard not to regard the tabloid press simply as predators in this context – keen to exploit any item of scandalous news to the full and at whatever cost to those concerned. From the point of view of the readership, though, there is clearly an audience for the revelations these tactics have produced, although it seems that there are limits even to that audience's ethical toleration of the tactics themselves (hence the furious reaction to the phone-hacking scandal from large cross-sections of the public). From a more pragmatic, industry-oriented, point of view, the tabloids' commercial power makes them almost irresistible as the quickest route to the public. They pitch so tirelessly to the consumer of celebrity that they offer an extraordinary commercial opportunity to anyone who can use them successfully. Consequently, and notwithstanding the repercussions of *The News of the World* scandal, the British tabloids continue to deal with the celebrity industries through a see-sawing pattern of scandalous exposures and negotiated exclusives – at one point threatening the professional survival of the celebrities they expose, and at another point contracting to provide them with unparalleled personal visibility. Little wonder that their mode of representation routinely works over the ambiguous territory between admiration and derision.

THE 'TABLOIDISATION' DEBATE

This brings us to the issue of what is called the 'tabloidisation' of the media – the critical domain within which the production of celebrity is most often discussed. As a phenomenon, and as we have seen, 'tabloidisation'[4] is most definitively located in sections of the British daily press, but the term has been extended to refer to a broad range of television formats as well. In the USA it includes muckraking current affairs programmes such as *A Current Affair*, 'reality TV' programmes such as *Cops*, and afternoon talk-confession shows such as *Oprah* and *Ricki Lake*. By its critics, the process of tabloidisation is usually considered to sacrifice information for entertainment, accuracy for sensation, and to employ tactics of representation which entrap and exploit its subjects (the hidden camera, the reconstruction, the ambush from the surprise talk-show guests). What are considered to be among its constitutive discourses range from the explicitly playful or self-conscious (the staged family conflicts, for instance, set up in *Ricki Lake*), to the self-important but bogus *gravitas* of the journalist exposing an issue of dubious 'public interest' (a politician's sex life, for instance). In practice, however, tabloidisation seems continually to expand as a category; it moves beyond the description of a particular kind of journalism to become a portmanteau description for what is regarded as the trivialisation of media content in general. As a term that accurately describes media formats and content, it is far too baggy, imprecise and value-laden to be useful as an analytic concept, in my view. However, it is a widely accepted label for a set of established debates about contemporary shifts in media content, production and consumption. As such, the production of celebrity through the media can be seen to fall under its ambit. I want to keep using the term 'tabloidisation' in what follows, then, as a convenient means of labeling those concerns that are conventionally collected under it.

Concern about tabloidisation is a routine topic for media commentators and pundits of all political persuasions. Customarily, tabloidisation is framed as a broad-based cultural movement, mostly visible in certain media forms, which is made possible by the increasing commercialisation of modern life and a corresponding decline in 'traditional values'. While this would suggest that the concept of tabloidisation expresses a conservative hostility to popular culture as a domain, it must be said that it also generates concern on the political left and among many with a professional interest in the media and popular culture. Todd Gitlin, for example, criticises the 'trivialisation of public affairs, the usurpation of public discourse by soap opera, the apparent breakdown of mechanisms for forming a public will and making it effective'. For him, 'trivialisation – infotainment and the like – works against the principled right and left alike' (1997: 35). His concern is echoed by the doyen of American communications scholars, James Carey:

> In recent years, journalism has been sold, to a significant degree, to the entertainment and information industries which market commodities globally that are central to the world economy of the twenty-first century. This condition cannot be allowed to persist ... The reform of journalism will only occur when the news organisations are disengaged from the global entertainment industries that increasingly contain them. (2002: 89)

The angry tone of Carey's piece indicates there is a moral or political dimension to his critique: it is not merely motivated by concern at shifts in the formal attributes of contemporary journalism. This is characteristic of critiques of tabloidisation (see Saltzman, 1999, for instance).

Alternative views have in turn attacked the moralistic nature of criticisms such as those outlined above, as well as their origin in elite conceptions of the public sphere. Ian Connell was severe on what he saw as the snobbery behind the criticism of tabloid journalism, and rejected the accusation that such journalism diverted us from more important political and social issues. Indeed, he argued that the tabloid's personalisation of news actually provided a more effective means of demonstrating the significance of the political:

> Contrary to what has often been claimed about the tabloid press, they are every bit as preoccupied with social differences and the tensions which arise from them as serious journalists or for that matter academic sociologists. The focus on personality and privilege is one of the ways in which these differences and tensions are represented as concrete and recognizable rather than as remote, abstract categories. (1992: 82)

It would have to be admitted that many of the concerns expressed about the influence of tabloidisation are grounded in a conventional and longstanding hostility to popular culture itself. Cultural studies has a rich tradition of revealing and challenging such a position. John Hartley's *Popular Reality* (1996) repeatedly attacks the class- and gender-based binarism that places information against entertainment, hard news against soft news, the public sphere against private lifestyles, and public service media against the commercial media. As Hartley says, such binarism has a long history as 'the common sense' of the media industry and among policy-makers, but that 'doesn't make it any the less prejudicial as a mental map of modern media':

> Not only do such binaries reinforce a systematic bias against popular, screen and commercial media, but they also tend to reinforce other prejudices, principally the one which considers many of the [denigrated terms in the opposition] as 'women's issues', with the (silent but inescapable) implication that serious politics and the public sphere is men's stuff. (1996: 27)

One of the key locations for what might be regarded as a moral panic about tabloidisation, and a location most directly associated with 'women's stuff', is the daytime television talk show. While some might condemn its 'Oprahfication' of America (see Shattuc, 1997: 86), others 'champion daytime talk shows as a new public sphere or a counter public sphere' (ibid.: 93). Far from stripping politics from the public arena, these are 'highly popular programs that depend on social topics and the participation of average citizens' (ibid.: 86). It is the access of such citizens to public debate that is so important in these accounts of the television talk show: crucially, these are citizens who have not hitherto enjoyed access to the television audience and whose voices have been silenced or ignored. As a result, Jane Shattuc claims that certain power structures are challenged by this form of television:

> The shows not only promote conversation but do away with the distance between audience and stage. They do not depend on the power of expertise or bourgeois education. They elicit common sense and everyday experience as the mark of truth. They confound the distinction between the public and the private. (1997: 93)

Shattuc does not make excessively liberatory claims for this form of entertainment, however. Ultimately, she concedes, these shows are neither intrinsically progressive nor intrinsically regressive. Gamson also highlights what he calls the 'paradoxes of visibility' enacted through these shows: they offer, he says, 'democratization through exploitation, truths wrapped in lies, normalization through freak show' (1998: 19). As he sees it, reflecting on his experience of guest appearances as an advocate of gay rights, these shows offer no choice between the 'manipulative spectacle and democratic forum' (ibid.: 19); you get both, no matter what. However, in their capacity to replicate the operation of the town meeting – the model Shattuc uses to explain their politics and human dynamics – they can be argued to offer a mode of participation that is implicitly democratic (ibid.: 94). Gamson is not likely to take such a view – as he says, 'if you have ever actually watched a few hours of talk shows, they seem as much about democracy as *The Price is Right* is about mathematics' (ibid.: 17) – but it deserves closer investigation. It is this 'implicitly democratic' function of the contemporary media I want to turn to next, more directly in relation to the media's construction of celebrity.

'DEMOCRATAINMENT'

As we saw in the previous chapter, the proliferation of opportunities for fame has been seen by some as a fundamentally liberatory development for the media in modern societies. The rise to media prominence of ordinary people, such as the contestants in *Big Brother* or the stars of the webcam sites, can be described as a new form of freedom. Leo Braudy directly compares modern celebrity with the forms of prominence or visibility that preceded it:

> [T]he longing for old standards of 'true' fame reflect a feeling of loss and nostalgia for a mythical world where communal support for achievement could flourish. But in such societies that did exist, it was always only certain social groups who had an exclusive right to call the tunes of glory, and other visual and verbal media were in the hands of a few. (1986: 585)

The older patterns of class and privilege have thus lost their power, he argues, and in its place is a new media democracy, where ordinary people now have greater access to media representation.

Furthermore, the consumers of celebrity are now able to play a part in the production of cultural visibility. According to Charles Leadbetter (2000), Princess Diana was 'created in part by her consumers': 'she was jointly owned by the people who consumed her image, the readers of *Hello!* magazine, the media and Diana herself' (2000: 25). Such an image is not employed in the unproblematic way assumed by the myths of earlier versions of 'true' fame. Instead, Gary Whannel suggests, public figures of 'spectacular celebritydom seem precisely to offer' their audiences 'modes of public exchange in which moral and political positionalities can be rehearsed' (2002: 214).

The most developed version of this kind of position is found in John Hartley's work, initially in his *Uses of Television* (1999), but also in more recent collections such as *The Uses of Digital Literacy* (2009). In the former, Hartley presents what has become a characteristically optimistic account of the popular media as they increasingly inform the construction of cultural identities through their performance of 'transmodern teaching': 'using "domestic discourses" to teach vast, unknowable, "lay" audiences modes of "citizenship" and knowledge based on culture and identity within a virtualized community of unparalleled size and diversity' (1999: 41).

That such a pedagogic practice should occur largely through the provision of entertainment is no impediment to its productive capacity. Breaking decisively with the paternalistic model of media provision identified with Reithian regimes of public broadcasting, the newly heterogeneous commercial media sphere offers the possibility of 'DIY citizenship': the construction of cultural identity through the operation of motivated media consumption. No longer restricted to a limited menu of mass media content, the DIY citizen has a multiplicity of choices available, offering identities through which they might construct their own. Hartley calls this process 'semiotic self-determination'. Informed by his principled rejection of elitist assumptions that might allocate aesthetic or moral values to particular media forms or genres of content, this is the world of 'democratainment'. There, the process of selection and choice in media consumption is held to structurally replicate the choices available to the free citizen in a democratic society. The evidence for such a possibility is found, with characteristic but pleasing perversity, precisely in the tabloidised forms so pilloried by other media commentators: television talk shows, fashion magazines, and the semiotic furniture of suburbia.[5]

It seems widely accepted in media and cultural studies that the more dispersed possibilities of production and distribution in the contemporary media – and not only through new technologies such as digital media – do imply the potential to achieve a 'different, less unequal vision of the mediated public sphere' (Couldry, 2003: 140) than seemed possible even a decade ago. Such a position is consistent with Braudy's much earlier (1986) description of the proliferation of celebrity and the disarticulation of fame from achievement as an intrinsically democratising force. It is also consistent with the defence of television talk shows we encountered earlier, which argues that these formats have brought new, previously marginalised, voices into the public sphere (Lumby, 1997; Masciarotte, 1991). This new diversity, in turn, argues Chris Rojek, results in the 'recognition and celebration of lifestyles, beliefs and forms of life previously unrecognised or repressed' (2001: 191). Hence there is a significant line of argument which suggests that, far from constituting an 'unrecognised threat to liberal democracy' (Schickel, 1985: 311), the media formats in question are a democratising force. And from one point of view, this would seem entirely self-evident. The celebrity offered to contestants through reality TV, contestants defined for us by their ordinariness, would certainly seem to constitute a more democratic phenomenon than a celebrity based on social, economic, religious or cultural hierarchies.

Frances Bonner, however, argues that there are limits to how 'ordinary' such people can be and thus to what extent we can see the spread of reality TV in particular as part of a democratising process. Even in TV's representation of the ordinary, there must be hierarchies. She points out that the contestants on game shows, reality TV and so on are exceptional in specific ways: television seeks those who can 'project a personality on television' and therefore some 'are more usefully ordinary than others' (2003: 53). Like a number of writers (for instance, Couldry, 2003), she reminds us that such shows employ a process of selection that has produced a particular, and motivated, construction of ordinariness for us to watch. It is in television's interest to mask and disavow this process. In its place, Bonner suggests (after Robert Stam) that television serves its 'inbuilt need to flatter the audience' by suggesting through the representation of ordinariness that they, too, belong on television. However, in fact, 'the people who appear ordinary on television' are 'just a little better looking, a little more articulate, a little luckier' (2003: 97) than the 'ordinary' we experience away from television.

Television's construction of the 'ordinary' is itself a category worth examining. Nick Couldry takes this next step in reference to *Popstars*:

> The ordinariness of these shows' contestants has a double significance in ritual terms: first, their 'ordinariness' confirms the 'reality' of what is shown (once their early performance strategies have, we assume, been stripped away by the continuous presence of the camera) and, second, that 'ordinariness' is the status from which the contestants compete to escape into another ritually distinct category, celebrity ... [this is] special, higher than the ordinary world. (2003: 107)

Couldry argues that there are in fact two kinds of people – 'media people' (those who are visible through the media) and 'ordinary people' – and that the distinction is hierarchical. The great value of celebrity is that it enables the 'ordinary' person to make the transition to being a 'media' person: that this is seen as an achievement – or a spectacular ritual in Couldry's terms – only reinforces the hierarchical structure which separates media people from ordinary people:

> So, in *Big Brother* and elsewhere, media rituals which seem to affirm the shared significance of an individual's transition to celebrity in fact entrench further the

working division between 'media people' and 'ordinary people'. Heavily ritualised processes such as media events which seem to affirm the shared significance of media institutions' picture of the world in fact insist upon the hierarchy of that picture over any possible other. (2003: 143)

Such arguments would suggest that the mere presence of the ordinary – a presence that has undeniably increased and is now firmly entrenched in programming formats on television – cannot be taken at face value.

Similarly, there are those who insist that the proliferation of social, gendered and ethnicised identities in the media generally cannot be seen as a democratising force, if only because of the larger ideological frame within which they are contained. Dovey claims that displays of deviance, such as those we might witness in a daytime talk show, 'actually serve to reinforce social norms by the individual pathologising of the speaker by the judging audience' (2002: 13), while Conboy argues that the characteristic action of the tabloid media in general is to 'close down into reaction' rather than open up 'into contestation' (2002: 149). It is possible to argue, on the other hand, that the relentlessness of this process has weakened significantly over the last couple of decades, and that the trends Hartley notices would constitute convincing evidence of the declining recalcitrance of such mechanisms of control and containment.

In his discussion of Hartley's *Uses of Television*, Couldry makes what seems to me a more telling criticism of the limits of the democratainment thesis. He acknowledges the justice of Hartley's proposition that the contemporary media, 'in its dispersed, and often ironic, form', sustain 'a public space in which the terms of public and private discourse are open to negotiation beyond formal political control' (Couldry, 2003: 18). That much, at least, seems to be conceded as a fair and reasonable account of the political possibilities released by the current configuration of the contemporary media, and it operates as a solid rebuttal to most aspects of the tabloidisation thesis. However, Couldry poses a fundamental question to Hartley, which defers the question about the effectivity of the DIY consumer by redirecting the debate towards the symbolic economy of the media itself. Hartley never addresses, Couldry says, the 'implications' for the democratainment thesis 'of the massive concentration of symbolic power in media institutions':

How does this affect our interpretation of the social 'uses' of television? Unless we rely on the jaded rhetoric of market liberalism, we can know nothing about the actual impacts, positive or negative, of contemporary media without considering, for example, the uneven symbolic landscape in which popular talk shows address their viewers and also their participants. (2003: 18)

It's a familiar debate within cultural studies, of course, issues of agency and determination recirculate continually. But it also reminds us of another familiar debate – between cultural studies and political economy – in that it insists the discussion of processes of consumption must first consider the conditions of production that determined what choices are actually on offer in the first place.

There has been considerable debate about these issues over the last decade, and as we have learnt more about how these new media forms function, and what kinds of consequences they appear to be delivering, there is considerably less enthusiasm for the idea of democratainment – precisely because of the connection it implies (but cannot demonstrate) between the broadening of media access, and the liberation of 'the ordinary' citizen from constrained menus of choice, with the principles of democracy (Couldry and Markham, 2007). I have taken this issue up myself in some detail in *Ordinary People and the Media: The Demotic Turn* (Turner, 2010), but the simple version can be put quite briefly. Those who argue that the last decade or so has witnessed the opening up of media access to women, to people of colour and to a wider array of class positions, are certainly right. However, this is more correctly seen as a demotic, rather than a democratic, development. There is no necessary connection between the widening of opportunities for participation we are now witnessing and a democratic politics: so, for instance, as I have noted elsewhere, the 'proliferation of blogs is not solely driven by progressive or liberal political attitudes – it houses extremism just as comfortably', and the media's 'interest in their reality and game show contestants is at least as exploitative as it is enabling' (2010: 1). At the structural level, no-one has yet even attempted to properly argue such a connection: it has simply been assumed. Or more correctly, there is a degree of theoretical slippage as the notion of semiotic self-determination through consumer choices within a liberalising market mutates into a more explicitly political version of self-determination. Diversity, wherever it occurs, it would seem, must be intrinsically democratic. It is worth reminding ourselves that in the media, at least, this diversity of consumer choice is achieved through the mechanism of price, rather than through a system of rights.

THE DEMOTIC TURN

Thus far I have been emphasising the pervasiveness of the influence of celebrity throughout the media, as well as the proliferation of the production of celebrity throughout the various media industries. To some extent, this is a story of the convergence of market strategies – with television, print and the internet, in particular, all milking the market opportunities available to them through the production, distribution and marketing of celebrity in one form or another. However, the multiplication of outlets, of formats and of the numbers of people subject to the discursive processes of 'celebrification', suggests a competing narrative: that of the opportunity of celebrity spreading beyond elites of one kind or another and into the expectations of the population in general. In conjunction with what seems like a widening of opportunity in this area, there is the proliferation of new sites of media production as well as the consolidation of non-traditional systems of delivery for media content – from cable television to Twitter (Marshall, 2010) – that we encountered in the previous chapter. Both of these trends have encouraged optimism about possible changes to the current concentration of ownership for major media forms. DIY production technologies are springing up to service DIY consumer-citizens, it would seem. As a result, it is not surprising that cultural studies researchers should suggest that increased powers of self-determination are now in the hands of media consumers – hence the democratic political possibilities read into the 'demotic turn'.

That there is a demotic turn seems to me beyond dispute. The media discourses used to represent 'ordinariness' edge closer every day towards the lived experience of 'the ordinary'. Ordinary people have never been more visible in the media, nor have their own utterances ever been reproduced with the faithfulness, respect and accuracy that they are today (Couldry, 2003: 102). The talk and confession genre of television delivers us raw, inflamed and spectacular performances of the ordinary every afternoon, while game shows spend millions trying to reproduce it. What constitutes the ordinary in the media, too, has been opened up dramatically to offer us multiple versions of class, gender, sexuality and ethnicity. At the same time, the range of media material now available for ordinary individuals to consume, assimilate and use is probably unparalleled. But the objective of this explosion of the ordinary does seem to me, as Couldry suggests and at least to some extent, to be an attempt to turn the representation of the ordinary into a kind of media ritual. What informs this is not necessarily what I would regard as the positive byproducts – the openness, the accessibility, the diversity, the recognition of marginalised citizens' rights to media representation. Rather, what motivates the media's mining of the ordinary seems to be their capacity to generate the performance of endless and unmotivated (and entertaining) diversity for its own sake. If this judgement is warranted, then the 'democratic' part of the 'democratainment' neologism is an accidental consequence of the 'entertainment' part and its least convincing component. It is important to remember that celebrity remains an hierarchical and exclusive phenomenon, no matter how much it proliferates. It is in the interests of those who operate this hierarchy in the contemporary context, however, to disavow its exclusivity; maybe what we are watching in the demotic turn is the celebrity industries' improved capacity to do this convincingly through the media.

For the individual celebrity, it might be possible to argue that, in the end, more opportunities are still more opportunities. Ordinary people can wind up on *Big Brother* or *Real Life* or a network soap opera just by the luck of the draw, and that possibility can certainly have its liberatory dimension (Andrejevic, 2004; Lumby, 2006). One would want to move, however, to an examination of specific cases to think about what actually occurs (see for instance, Allen, 2011). In our research on celebrity in Australia, Frances Bonner, David Marshall and I found that the less connected the achievement of celebrity was to some training, performance background or the like – in fact, the more arbitrary it was – the less equipped the person concerned was to handle the inevitable discovery that their fame had nothing to do with them and that it could disappear overnight. The housemates on *Big Brother*, by and large, will not generate careers in the public eye; the young soap stars on *Neighbours*, by and large, will drift out of the industry as they are unable to find roles in anything more rewarding than regional British Christmas pantomimes. In such a situation, we felt, a key issue was the level of responsibility accepted by the promotions and publicity personnel who represented these celebrities and traded their commodity status while it had value. Many of those personnel shared that view and expressed concern about the destructive cycle of discovery, exploitation and disposal that was fundamental to the way their industries used individual stars.

The reason for such a cycle is the pursuit of profit by large internationalised media conglomerates who, despite the demotic turn in representation and consumption, still control the symbolic economy. Notwithstanding the proliferation of DIY celebrities online, and the availability of digital production technologies in all kinds of media forms, this is still in the same hands it has always been. It might be seductive to think of the internet as an alternative, counter-public sphere – and in many ways its chaotic contents would support such a view. But it is still a system that is dominated by white, middle-class, American men, and increasingly integrated into the major corporate structures of the traditional media conglomerates.

What is new, however, is that we seem to be witnessing a new process of identity formation as media content mutates. Celebrity is playing an increasingly important role, I would argue, in these new modes of production of cultural identity. Relevant here is P. David Marshall's (2010) proposition that we are now embedded in a 'presentational culture', where the production or presentation of the public self has become the focus of intense engagement – particularly among young people, and particularly through social media or what Marshall describes as 'presentational media' (2010: 35). Celebrity provides the model for the production of this kind of self. As it is increasingly used in this way, the meaning of celebrity itself begins to mutate: from being an elite and magical condition to being an almost reasonable expectation from everyday life. Certainly, the consumption of celebrity has become a part of everyday life in the twenty-first century, and so it is not surprising if it now turns up as part of young people's life-plans (Hopkins, 2002). It is important to understand this shift.

In most respects my personal sympathies lie with the more optimistic and populist accounts of shifts in popular culture: when one sees who is presenting the more conservative case, it makes one suspect the interests it might serve. However, it is important to recognise that it is easy to overstate the democratic potential of the new media systems and formats. Reality TV has presented us with some interesting moments in media performance, and the spectacle of 'everyday life', no matter how it is produced, can make for some compelling television. However, the industrial cycle of use and disposal mentioned above does seem to have radically accelerated in response to the demand created by new media forms. This suggests the activity of a process of increased commodification rather than enhanced political enfranchisement. As Marshall demonstrates in such detail in *Celebrity and Power* (1997), the interests served are first of all those of capital, and nothing has changed this so far.

That said, it is all too easy to slide into a moralising political critique of the forms of celebrity, of the artificiality of the cultural status it appears to confer, and of the media forms that carry its related products. To do this, I absolutely accept, would be to greatly underestimate the complexity of these forms and products as well as the varied cultural and social functions they might perform. Further, it would divert us from discussing what I would regard as the more important and interesting aspects of the modern phenomenon of celebrity. It is not the perceived triviality of the talk show or the celebrity magazine, nor even the extraordinary range of media forms the production of celebrity has adopted, that attracts *my* central interest. Rather, it is the fact that celebrity now occupies an increasingly significant role in the process through which we construct our cultural identities. As we move, then, from the production side of this analysis in Part 2 to the consumption side in Part 3, it is to the social and cultural function of celebrity that I want to turn my attention.

NOTES

1 Like many of the celebrity weeklies, *Hello!* retains remnants of the traditional women's magazine: beauty hints, recipes and fashion.

2 *Hello!* is particularly interesting in this regard. Far more respectable than any of its counterparts in the USA, for instance, it offers an attractive reader demographic to advertisers. According to its website, it is the only mass circulation women's magazine (that is the category into which the circulation survey places it, and indeed 80 per cent of its readers are women) with nearly one-third of its readers falling into the upmarket AB demographic.

3 This is the increasingly accepted way of describing a global media product that conforms to a branded international format, but is localised in terms of its specific content. So the various national editions of *FHM* or *Vogue* may represent a franchising of the brand but each may contain substantially different editorial content from the other.

4 The discussion of tabloidisation in this section draws heavily upon Turner (1999) where some of these arguments were first developed, and where some of the complications unable to be integrated into this account are discussed at greater length.

5 The ordinary person who becomes a celebrity is perhaps the epitome of what can be achieved through this semiotic self-determination (although this is achieved through gaining access to the processes of production as well as those of consumption).

Part three

Consumption

5   The Cultural Function of Celebrity

At times [celebrities] are part of the background noise and flow – part of the wallpaper, we say – and at times they loom up as something more. Sometimes we evaluate them as physical beings and moral agents. Often we find them desirable, or enviable, or in some other way they evoke the sentiments, the liking, irritation or boredom, that flesh and blood individuals evoke. Yet an aura of some sort surrounds them. They take up ritual places as heroes, leaders, scapegoats, magical figures, to be admired, envied, loved or hated: to matter. (Gitlin, 2001: 132)

CELEBRITY 'FROM BELOW'

This chapter sets out to provide an answer to the question: what is the cultural function of celebrity? It is a question that has been around for a long time but gained added significance in the wake of the extraordinary spectacle of the international popular reaction to the death of Diana, Princess of Wales, in 1997. Before Diana's death, it may have been possible to dismiss the 1990s explosion of celebrity content, the arrival of the mass market for celebrity gossip and even the particular form of celebrity that Diana enjoyed, as relatively ephemeral cultural shifts. Those who might have done so, however, were suddenly confronted with what appeared to be genuine sadness expressed by those who were complete strangers to the woman who had died, but who felt that they knew her as part of their lives. At such a point, the precise cultural function performed by a figure such as Diana seemed to be in urgent need of examination.

One of the consequences of a globalised media delivered via many different platforms is that contemporary media visibility is potentially exorbitant in scale. The intensity of the competition between cable and terrestrial television means that high profile news stories are top priorities for the whole industry.[1] Accordingly, CNN will cover a breaking story live for hours, competing with FOX, BBC World and Al-Jazeera (just for starters) as it does so, and news sites on the internet will stream live video drawn from the mobile phones of witnesses and participants alike. Of course, there have always been 'flashpoints' in popular culture, where a particular event or person completely dominates media coverage, producing 'an excessively focused global public' (Turner et al., 2000: 4). Diana's death was such a flashpoint, and remains one of the most extreme cases; as we described it in *Fame Games*, it was 'simply uncontainable as news, as obituary, as identity politics, as entertainment, as myth or narrative, or as gossip' (ibid.: 4). The scale of the media presence indicated something about the enhanced capacities of the global media at the time, but more important was its demonstration of the power of the relationship between mass-mediated celebrities and the consumers of popular culture. Notwithstanding the fact that the relationship between Diana and her public had certainly been produced, spindoctored and managed to the nth degree, the emotions generated by her death forced the relationship to break free of its management – to become, as it were, an unequivocally 'real' event. At that point, 'the potential of the modern audience's relationship with a person they know solely through their media representations, but who nevertheless plays a part in their lives', was made 'vividly, if bewilderingly, apparent' (ibid.: 4).

Of course, the popular mourning of a public figure across national boundaries is not unprecedented. We can think of the funeral of John F. Kennedy, or the international reaction to the death of John Lennon. Anthony Elliott's description of the response to the death of John Lennon usefully reminds us of the scale of the 'global mourning' which accompanied that event:

> On Sunday, 14 December, 1980 [six days after his death], an estimated crowd of one hundred thousand people joined together in silence in New York's Central Park to remember John Lennon. Others around the world did likewise. A gathering of thirty thousand people joined in prayer and sang 'Give Peace a Chance' outside St George's Hall on Lime Street in Liverpool. In cities across America, vigils were held to commemorate the life and work of Lennon. In Toronto, thirty-five thousand people gathered in snow for a candlelight vigil. Tens of thousands stopped to mourn Lennon in Paris, Hamburg, Madrid, Brussels, London, Melbourne and other major cities. In terms of public grief, nothing like it had been seen before. As for the media coverage, while there was no CNN or BBC World to take it up, *Time*, *Newsweek* and the *Sunday Times* devoted issues to his death, there were television and radio specials, and his most recent album *Double Fantasy* returned to the top of the charts, remaining at number one for eight weeks, and still in the top 100 eighteen months later. (1999: 143)

The difference perhaps, between Kennedy and Lennon on the one hand and Diana on the other, is that it was probably easy to assume that Diana didn't *matter*. Kennedy's death was a major political event from any point of view and John Lennon was one of the most famous and successful musicians of all time. Gender, presumably, also played a role here. Whatever the reasons, however, one could have been forgiven for thinking, before her death, that Diana was celebrated merely for her spectacular visibility, for the soap opera of her failed fairy-tale marriage, and for the beauty of her image. The public response to her death suggested otherwise.

In the previous chapter, I used the phrase 'the demotic turn' to describe the expansion of consumers' choice in their media diet, in general, and, in particular, the proliferation of the opportunities for the participation of 'ordinary people' in contemporary media. There is a demotic aspect here, too; the reaction to Diana's death revealed the grassroots existence of modes of relating to such a celebrity, which really had not made it onto the radar of most cultural criticism. The conditions were always there, of course, in the paradox I referred to earlier in the discussion of the production of celebrity: that while whole industries devote themselves to producing celebrity, the public remains perfectly capable of expressing their own desires as if the production industry simply did not exist. Gilbert Rodman accurately diagnoses this condition in his discussion of the ubiquity and longevity of the cult of Elvis Presley, decades after Elvis's death:

> [S]tardom is not a purely mercantile phenomenon imposed 'from above' by profit-hungry media conglomerates as much as it is a socially based phenomenon generated 'from below' at the level of real people who make affective investments in particular media figures … [T]he cultural circulation of Elvis as an icon has moved beyond the power of big business to control it: today, the people who wield the most power over Elvis's public image are the millions of individuals across the globe who are his fans. (1996: 12–13)

Celebrity 'from below', then, is a mode of consumption, and it is powerful. And, as we saw in the discussion of social media earlier on, it is becoming more powerful.

Such arguments take seriously the relationship between the celebrity and those who consume their images and the stories about them. As was apparent in the flurry of newspaper opinion page ponderings after Diana's death, however, not everyone saw it like this. In the Afterword written for his post-Diana revision of *Intimate Strangers* in 2000, Richard Schickel, for instance, talks about the 'illusion of intimacy' that might connect us with Diana or Lennon or Kennedy, suggesting that the 'cynically fostered relationship' constructed between Diana and the public 'resides only in the minds of the beholders'. Those in charge of manipulating the image – Diana and her minders – know that 'none really exists' (2000: 303.) While not everyone would put it as bluntly as this, there is a degree of reluctance to regard the celebrity-consumer relationship – despite its contemporary pervasiveness – as a normal component of modern social relations. Even those who obviously find the relationship intrinsically interesting and have written about it at length – Joshua Gamson, for instance, or Toby Young – reveal an underlying (and in Gamson's case, only initial) lack of respect for it in odd ways. In both these cases, their books include a surprising confession: that due to what they consider to be their relative sophistication, they are shocked by how thoroughly they have been sucked in by celebrity, how they have been drawn into a relationship almost against their better selves. As Gamson puts it, plaintively, 'what were these people doing in my life? … I was a PhD candidate from an established family!' (1994: 4).

The assumptions that inform reactions such as these are based on a conviction that because the celebrity-consumer relationship is constructed through the media it is also ultimately inauthentic – a surrogate for something more genuine. This point of view is reflected in the tradition of explanation that describes the relevant relations of consumption as para-social. It is this conceptualisation of the relationship between the celebrity figure and their public that I want to address in the following section.

THE PARA-SOCIAL RELATIONSHIP

> Consider the special skills of cultish fans. They construct para-social, imagined connections to celebrities or actants, who fulfil friendship functions or serve as spaces for projecting and evaluating schemas that make sense of human interaction. (Miller et al., 2001: 174–5)

Describing the interaction, and by extension the relationship, between fans or consumers and celebrities as para-social has a reasonably long history. In her discussion of this approach, Joli Jenson refers back to the work of Horton and Wohl in 1956, where fandom is described as a surrogate relationship, 'one that inadequately imitates normal relationships'. Jenson argues that such a construction pathologises the fan-celebrity relationship as potentially abnormal, containing the seeds for the obsessive pursuit of a more direct relationship (1992: 16–17). Further, framed in such a way, para-social interaction is in danger of being used as a substitute for other kinds of social participation, again carrying the seeds for aberrant behaviour:

> To be a fan, Schickel and others imply, is to attempt to live vicariously, through the perceived lives of the famous. Fandom is conceived of as a chronic attempt to compensate for a perceived personal lack of autonomy, absence of community, incomplete identity, lack of power and lack of recognition. (ibid.: 17)

A logical outcome of this is disturbed or obsessional behaviour. Since Schickel believes that the celebrity with whom the fan has a relation is in fact a fiction – 'a creature carelessly constructed for them, against the rush of a thousand deadlines, out of gossip' (2000: 303) – it is not surprising he has little faith in the sociability of the relation. He is not alone, though, in seeing only differences of scale between the more everyday form of celebrity consumption (that is, the kind of thing we might indulge in ourselves), and the psychopathic fixation on individual celebrities that has produced stalking and even assassination. Rojek suggests 'isolated and lonely people are vulnerable to developing what Horton and Wohl refer to as "extreme para-sociability" with certain presenters'. As a result, their 'fantasies of intimacy and solidarity' with these presenters can 'carry over' into their primary personal relationships, their delusions of connection producing 'unhealthy neuroses and morbid obsessions' (2012: 125.) It is this kind of view that Jenson's article challenges.

Rojek's argument in *Fame Attack* has a particular goal in mind – an unblinkered consideration of the social consequences of celebrity – that motivates his approach to para-social relations (he devotes a full chapter to discussing this issue). However, he would acknowledge that this approach does run slightly against the grain of what has become more commonly a less perjorative account of fandom or the consumption of celebrity in the current media environment. Elliott, for instance, describes fandom as 'a process of self-constitution, of enriching the self' (1999; 139). Giles might not go that far but he also presents a more positive reading of the para-social relationship than the accounts Jensen critiques. Giles himself, with a background in the behavioural sciences from which this idea originates, adopts conventional usage by claiming that para-social interactions are substitutes for 'real relationships', a proposition he says is clearly demonstrated by the use of pornography (2000: 65). Nevertheless, he has reservations about the suitability of applying the term to the consumption of celebrity. It is wrong, he argues, to use the same term to describe the relationship we construct between ourselves and 'real' people and those we might construct in our imagination between ourselves and characters in a movie. While celebrities might be relatively inaccessible, they are nonetheless living beings 'with whom a bilateral relationship is possible' (ibid · 129) and the wish that this might occur is not an especially irrational desire. Furthermore, the term 'para-social interaction' does not accurately describe the kind of relationship listeners might enjoy with, for instance, celebrity broadcasters, who they might never meet but with whom they might talk (sometimes) daily – and nor, as suggested in Chapter 3, does it cover the kind of relationship a fan might develop while following and engaging with their favourite celebrity's Twitter feed. Finally, Giles suggests, it is increasingly the case that the kinds of relations we might describe as para-social are routinely encountered in a society where certain dimensions of family and community relations have shrunk:

> As the research on para-social interaction suggests, many people use television as a way of combating loneliness; with a trend towards single living, particularly among young people, the uses and gratifications of para-social relationships may become increasingly important as society fragments further. (ibid.: 148)

Rojek (2001) makes a similar point in his first book on celebrity, when he admits that while para-social interaction refers to a form of 'second-order intimacy' – that is, 'relations of intimacy constructed through the mass media rather than direct experience and face-to-face meetings' – it is an increasingly common feature of everyday life. 'Nonetheless', he says, 'in societies in which as many as 50 per cent of the population confess to sub-clinical feelings of isolation and loneliness, para-social interaction is a significant aspect of the search for recognition and belonging'. In response to this need, celebrities, Rojek continues, 'offer peculiarly powerful affirmations of belonging, recognition and meaning' (ibid.: 52). He also points out that the social and physical remoteness of the celebrity (the crucial aspect in describing the level of intimacy as second-order) is massively compensated in the contemporary world by the amount of contact – highly personal contact – available through mass-mediated representations. The assumptions easily made in the 1950s about our relation to media figures need to be revised in a context where the media now play a significantly different role.

Rojek (2012) makes a further contribution to that revision himself. While he does canvas the possibility of the destructive potential of 'extreme para-sociability', he has a number of other concerns about behaviour that is not so extreme. Among them is how what he calls the 'para-social conversations' generated by celebrity operate as a form of 'life-coaching', providing 'free advice about grooming, impression management, self-promotion and even "correct" social, political, cultural and environmental values' (2012: 139). This advice, he argues, 'carries over into ordinary life as a resource that equips individuals to present themselves as more relevant, competent and capable':

> Thus, star power provides cultural capital of lifestyle coaching that is directly transferable to everyday life. Para-social relationships are important in culture, not just as vehicles for narcissistic idealization and hero worship, but they are also used practically to enhance the presentation of personality, refine lifestyle skills and expand social appeal. (ibid.:139)

Interestingly, the positive cultural power this cedes to the celebrity also has a negative side:

> Para-social conversations are just as dangerous to some isolated and vulnerable stars as they are to isolated, vulnerable ordinary people. For they make the star look into the mirror of public adoration and media applause and see the reflection of an untouchable being. But this reflection is a mirage. Stars who are consistently heedless of public opinion or engage in recorded narcissistic outbursts walk on the edge of a cauldron. (ibid.:141)

As examples of the celebrity who has allowed themselves to believe the 'mirage', and develop an exaggerated sense of narcissistic entitlement, Rojek cites Kanye West's notorious intervention in the awarding of an MTV award to singer Taylor Swift in 2009, and Mel Gibson's menacing phone calls to Oksana Grigorievan in 2010.

Finally, it is also important that we consider these relationships from the point of view that regards them as spiritual rather than social. John Frow proposes that 'the form of apotheosis associated with the modern star system is a phenomenon of a strictly religious order' (1998: 201). All the trappings are there around the dead Elvis, Diana and Jim Morrison: the shrines, memorials, regular gatherings of the faithful, even sightings of the reincarnation – all signs of a religious practice. The only reason, says Frow, that this has not been examined in some detail is that cultural studies has ignored religious experience and is therefore ill-equipped methodologically to pursue this question productively. This despite the fact that religious sentiment has 'migrated into many strange and unexpected places, from New Age trinketry to manga movies and the cult of the famous dead' (ibid.: 207–8). As noted in Chapter 1, Rojek, in both his books on celebrity, also spends a considerable amount of time dealing with celebrity as a religious practice.

The term 'para-social', then, may be useful in highlighting the difference between face-to-face relations and those provided through the media, but there are limitations to the usefulness of the term as a means of describing the quality and cultural function of such relations. Most of the more recent evidence on the consumption of celebrity would suggest a far more fundamental – be it social, cultural or even religious – function being served than is consistent with descriptions that see it as a merely compensatory, second-order practice. That would certainly seem to be the lesson to be taken from the mourning of Diana.

ROYAL CELEBRITY

As Chris Rojek indicates in his typology of celebrity, royalty is one of the few modes of celebrity that is determined by blood: in his terms, it is 'ascribed celebrity'. Royalty inherit their prominence and with it the (mostly) 'automatic respect and veneration' due to their structural role in the architecture of the state. As Rojek puts it, individuals 'may add or subtract from their ascribed status by virtue of their voluntary actions, but the foundation of their ascribed celebrity is predetermined' (2001: 17). They are, then, protected from many of the vicissitudes experienced by celebrities from the entertainment, media and sports industries. Where the celebrity from the entertainment world is subject to shifts in fashion and taste that can wipe out their professional careers completely, the royal celebrity's continuity is more or less assured. They may move in and out of the public gaze, take a more or less active role in public life, but they will continue to occupy the same status for life. The guarantee of privilege, of course, runs against the grain of the last couple of centuries of democratic politics, so there is a great deal of representational work required to negotiate that contradiction. As a result, royalty seeks a presence in mass-market magazines such as *Hello!*, requiring the same kind of involvement with publicity and public relations that we might associate with party politics or the movie industry. The maintenance of an explicitly elite hereditary institution within a democratic state requires some management and the offering of individual members for consumption as celebrities has been one of the strategies employed. In recent years in the UK, the specifics of this mode of public relations have emphasised the ordinariness, the everyday knowable-ness of the royal family, as a means of disavowing the hierarchical structure which keeps them in place.

Such an account might suggest that the British public is the object of something of a public relations con trick, however the evidence tends to point the other way. Michael Billig's much admired book, *Talking of the Royal Family* (1992), demonstrates that his respondents were not duped or misled by the exorbitance of the publicity they consume or the stories they read about the royal family. Instead, Billig suggests that the public appreciates the royal family as a form of spectacular entertainment, a particular form of public life that is offered for their enjoyment. As David Chaney points out, people seem to understand that the 'majesty' of royalty is constructed and that its display is deliberately managed. Like Billig, Chaney says that the public understanding of this fact makes the display itself 'all the more real, rather than less real' as a result (2001: 215). Billig's book is a fundamental resource on the specificity of the public meanings connected to the British royal family and it demonstrates how fully integrated they are into his respondents' everyday lives. The dialectics between the domestic and the public, between the ordinary and the extraordinary, are played out in these family conversations where observations on the activities of the royal family are routinely turned into conversations about the ethics and practices of everyday life. As a result, Chaney says, the British royal family can be regarded as 'a sort of mirror in which competing versions of Britishness as well as everyday gendered and family identities are overlappingly articulated' (ibid.: 208).

Nonetheless, there are significant obstacles to be overcome for this process to succeed. While it is a heavily naturalised role that the royal family performs, it is also the most aggressively exclusive of all forms of celebrity (Couldry, 2001: 223). It is denied the forms of legitimation available to film stars or television personalities, for instance: there is no narrative of discovery, no invocation of magical talent, no 'star quality' explaining the sudden rise to fame. The royals lack a legitimating myth of success. This is where Diana comes in. Her celebrity produced 'a curious variant of the myth of success': she was a commoner,[2] a misfit, and ultimately 'a failure in her royal duties' from the perspective of most of the family (ibid.: 230).

The specificity of the celebrity inhabited by the royal family both ensured Diana's exceptional prominence – as the modernising influence, the new blood, as 'populism in trainers' (ibid.: 225) – and her automatic incorporation into the everyday life of the British people. At the same time, and because of her crucial points of difference from the rest of the royal family, she developed a specificity of her own that enabled her to intersect in strategic ways with mainstream celebrity discourse. Diana provides a link to mainstream/entertainment celebrities because unlike most of the royal family she was not born into it: she could be understood through a narrative of discovery, good fortune and the like, much in the way a Hollywood star might be. The narrative does not stop there, however, as it continues to parallel the Hollywood story throughout her life. Where the faded Hollywood star, we might be told, was destroyed by the careless venality of an industry uninterested in her particular qualities, the story of Diana has her used and traduced in order to serve the interests of the monarchy itself. Her popularity was clearly enhanced by revelations of the royal family's growing impatience with her resistance to the traditions within which she was ensnared. This had the simultaneous effect of undermining the legitimacy of the institution and of turning her 'commoner' origins into an heroic attribute. It is not hard to see why she became a point of focus for debates about the state of the British polity during her lifetime and a rallying point for anti-monarchist sentiment after her death.

Rather than operating simply as a sad anachronism within the royal family – a tragically misplaced pop celebrity – Diana's celebrity was built through a complex relationship to the conventional forms of royal celebrity (where she was already part of something that mattered to the nation) and the mobilisation of discourses of populism and a constructed 'ordinariness'. At a cultural moment when it is the ordinary rather than the elite that is in the discursive ascendancy, the rest of the royal family probably never had a chance in the competition for the public interest and it seems the public would not forgive them for failing to realise that.

MOURNING DIANA

> If mourning Diana was a hugely over-determined event, its ruptural character was secured by two main eventualities. The first ... was simply her dying – her dying as she did, when she did. The second ... was Diana's extraordinary availability as a figure for the identity work of others. (Johnson, 1999: 23)

The public mourning of Diana, Princess of Wales, has been excessively scrutinised, analysed and discussed (see for example, Campbell, 1998; Kear and Steinberg, 1999; Re:Public, 1997). Many were surprised by the public expression of emotion that was, in most people's memory, unprecedented. Others were surprised by what they regarded as the public's gullibility; to them, the outpouring of emotion was bogus, the product of media orchestration. While, for some, Diana's particular form of celebrity was what attracted their interest and affection, for others it was precisely this celebrity which made it unthinkable that anyone should respond to her as if she was a 'real person'. Many intellectuals on the left, in particular, experienced this as an extremely discomforting and puzzling phenomenon, and they found it difficult to sympathise with the mourners or understand their grief as anything but some curious form of mass delusion. Others, such as Beatrix Campbell (1998), took the opportunity to explain why this phenomenon was not just a media event and how it might be perceived as, in its own way, political.

In cultural studies the puzzlement was palpable. Already aligned around varied positions on what used to be called cultural populism (McGuigan, 1992), far from united over how to read the cultural politics of celebrity and understandably suspicious of a public agenda that seemed identical with the promotional strategies of the tabloid press, there was not an obvious response for cultural studies to make. Nonetheless, they entered the fray with some vigour. Diana died in August 1997 and before the year was out the Australian collective Re:Publica (which included Ien Ang, Helen Grace, Ruth Barcan, Elaine Lally and Justine Lloyd) had published an edited collection called *Planet Diana: Cultural Studies and Global Mourning* aimed directly at analysing the crisis of comprehension within cultural studies that Diana's death had created. *Screen*, a journal perhaps not known for its engagement in the flashpoints of popular culture, also devoted a special issue to the debate (1998, 39(1), and it ran on into subsequent issues as well). The collection of essays in *Screen* also revealed significant disagreement about the nature of the events the contributors had witnessed. Interestingly, as well, the editor, Annette Kuhn, admitted in her preface to some concern about the inappropriateness for this task of the kind of writing her contributors were used to producing. Consequently, Kuhn said, all of her contributors were 'aware of the challenge involved in applying [their] skills to a phenomenon of such extraordinary cultural weight'. This was further complicated by the significant fact that the special debate in *Screen* was not just a work of analysis, it was also 'an act of mourning in the classic sense' (Kuhn, 1998: 67).

Fundamental to so much of the academic debate was the view that Diana was a figure who had been massively mediated in her representation and, therefore, the public response to her death was itself inevitably compromised – as if such a response was always already illegitimate. Equally fundamental was the contrary perception – picked up accurately (albeit often quite uncomfortably) by academics committed to understanding popular culture's meanings and pleasures – that those who had responded so emotionally to her death could not be simply dismissed as the dupes of media manipulation. For one thing, and aside from theoretical considerations involved here, it was not hard to recognise that the movement was too broad-based for that. Not only were the mourners broadly representative of a cross-section of the community – at least in London on the evidence of attendance at the funeral event – but they also included substantial pockets of groups identified with marginalised or minority positions (gay men, people of colour, for instance). These were hardly the groups one would expect to uncritically absorb media messages or to unthinkingly adopt mass-mediated attitudes towards the establishment.

Curiously, the debates about the authenticity versus the mediated character of the event reflect something of a failure for some in media and cultural studies to properly understand the media's role in performing public events for the imagined community – of the nation, certainly, but also in this instance for a global audience united in their response to Diana's death. Karin Becker, in her contribution to the *Screen* debates (1998), draws attention to the naivety of thinking that there is media and there is reality, that we can easily separate the two into the representation and the real, and that one is wholly authentic while the other is not. In the case of media events, it was apparently necessary to say, it may be that there is no other reality than that which is provided through the media. A media event such as Diana's funeral is no less 'real' just because it is a media event. As Becker puts it, in such instances, 'there is no place outside the event for the media to stand and merely document, as in the idealized version of the journalist's stance':

> In this case, the media were not only integral to the extraordinary events surrounding Diana's death, but actually constituted the cultural performance of her funeral as a collective ritual response of mourning. (1998: 292)

This is a useful corrective to idealist assumptions about the public function of the media, but Becker's argument also helps recover the importance of the private processing of this ritual. Emphasising that such an event is not unique in character but simply massive in scale, she describes a much more persuasive model of the actual process of participation involved than those offered by simple notions of thoughtless media consumption or, worse, mass hysteria:

> Diana's death and the events leading up to the funeral were not events that people watched and 'consumed' so much as participated in, via the media, as well as through other private and public forms of documentation and commemoration. [...] I argue that the media work not as appropriators of some presumably genuine public emotion and participation, but as collaborators, co-constructors, inseparable from a public 'response' in the interweaving of phenomena and the meanings that accrue to them in the formation and enactment of the rituals of contemporary life. (ibid.: 289)

If this sounds a little optimistic, there are other accounts that accept the media's implication in the production of everyday life, but which do not necessarily see them as 'collaborators' with the public in the production of meaning. McGuigan's account acknowledges a form of partnership between the media and the public, the kind of trade in representations and meanings that Becker refers to, when he describes Diana as a site of 'affective communication and public disputation over the conduct of life' (McGuigan, 2000: 11). Diana is at the centre of one spectacular instance of how the mass media, through their exploitation of celebrity and scandal, may actually 'facilitate as well as distort popular deliberation on the conduct of life' (ibid.: 16). Fully aware of the professional activities of the media, the spin-doctors and the publicists, McGuigan nonetheless points out that this is not confined to the production of celebrity. If the affective relations between Diana and her mourners are subject to media manipulation, then this is also true of the full range of relations that make up the imagined community of any of the nations in which we live. Reminiscent of the arguments Hartley makes in *Popular Reality* (1996), and far from seeing the media as occupying an antithetical role to that of the public, McGuigan points out that we need the media to bring the imagined community (or as Hartley would have it, the public) into being: 'the only way that imagined community ... can be constructed in modern times, especially at short notice, [is] through the instantaneity of the media, press, and, most importantly, television' (2000: 13). We live in a world of mass-mediated relationships and these have changed the character and constitution of everyday life. However, it is also worth noting that a number of commentators have argued against the media conspiracy thesis by pointing out that, far from orchestrating the response to Diana's death, the media seemed as puzzled and as wrong-footed as anyone else by the grass-roots character of the reactions they had to cover and explain.

One of the most impressive attempts to understand the event and the intensity of his own emotional reaction to it was written by Richard Johnson (1999). Like so many others, Johnson admits both his puzzlement at the global mourning and his sympathy with the emotions he saw being expressed around him. In what is a very personal essay, Johnson sets out to explain what is going on by examining his own reaction – in particular, how closely entwined it was with the grief he had experienced since his wife died. The self-reflexivity he employs to demonstrate how these two deaths became enmeshed in his own life shows very clearly how one could react to Diana's death as if it was to someone who had played a part in one's own everyday life.

Johnson admits at the outset that he was 'moved by Diana's death and by the actions of the other mourners' and 'caught by surprise' by his own tears. Although he suspected he might have 'learned to cry too easily' since his wife died, he also realised that there were 'convergencies' between the two situations – that of his wife's death and that of Diana's death – and a significant degree of transference of his feelings between the two. As a result, he was sympathetic to 'mourning Diana', especially to its eruptive excessiveness; more sympathetic, he notes, than many of his academic colleagues (1999: 18). This was not simply an intellectual weakness, or a form of emotionalism, however. Although he is perfectly aware of the transience of this grief and of the 'massively mediated' nature of Diana as a public figure, he argues cogently that this should not make a significant theoretical difference; this experience was genuine:

> Yet I disagree with critics of the mourning who make an in-principle distinction between 'face-to-face' and more 'mediated' mourning, between for instance, 'the death of someone who was actually a friend and the more ethereal loss of someone known only as a media figure' (Wilson, 1997: 136). It is not clear why

mourning with a mediated aspect must be more 'ethereal', less real. For many Diana mourners and not only those who had met her face-to-face, mourning was 'real' enough to produce significant actions and discussions within everyday spaces. Similarly, Diana's celebrity, even her privilege, does not in itself inauthenticate the feelings woven around her. (1999: 18)

A number of other writers on this subject took the view that because the object of their grief was a popular celebrity this necessarily devalued the feelings they experienced. What Johnson demonstrates is how our feelings for the popular celebrity are incorporated into what he calls 'identity work'.

What becomes interesting as a result is not Diana's media production, the epidemic of representation that accompanied her every move, but her widespread imbrication into the public's resources for the production of meaning, pleasure and identity. This is enhanced by her unusual discursive 'availability' to the public. She was available, says Johnson, not just as a glossy image but also as a representative of a shifting definition of British identity; as a mechanism of recognition for others who were marginalised or displaced within the society; as the object of 'a continuous play of identification and dis-identification'; and as the object of transferred feelings; 'feelings that had little to do with her own life and death, and everything to do with the lives of members of her public' (ibid.: 24–33). Johnson argues that it is as a result of this availability – 'for others to invest in as a source of pleasure, identity and recognition' (ibid.: 36) – that Diana was mourned so intensely:

She combined a powerful redefinition of a traditional (royal) representative function with the ability to acknowledge something of the reality of other people's lives, especially those suffering from major oppressions and ill-fortune. This endeared her to large numbers of people, especially those who had endured formative experiences of grief and subordination in their own lives. The widespread identifications, face-to-face or through media which always sought to possess even her private selves, set the terms of a passionate, political mourning. Even in her death, Diana bequeathed to others the opportunity to grieve for ungrieved bereavements of their own. Misrecognized by critics as manufactured or sentimental, this mourning was a typical expression of public grief and personal loss, magnified as much by the intimacy and extent of Diana's social connections (face-to-face and mediated) as by modern global media themselves. (ibid.: 37)

I have stayed with the example of Diana for the bulk of this chapter because of what I regard as its exemplary function – not just for this book, but for all of us who examine the workings of popular cultural forms. It seems to me one of the signal moments when what had been comfortably accepted within so much of the field as a para-social relation – a surrogate for more direct relations – behaved as if it was in fact a thoroughly *social* relation. Despite the growing interest in celebrity within cultural studies at the time, few of us would have predicted the character of the relationships exposed after Diana's death. And so, a common element in the reaction to her death and to its mourning was surprise that the cultural function of the celebrity became so dramatically evident the moment the news broke. As Johnson says, it is inaccurate to regard this as a media beat-up. What produced the shocking initial response was simply the fact of her death, and then, the way she died. The mediated ruminations upon that death, the retrospectives and evaluations of her life, came afterwards and were always hurrying to catch up with the popular mood. The celebrity of Diana, the 'People's Princess', stands then as an exceptionally powerful demonstration that the contemporary mass-mediated public figure plays a role in our lives that has been misunderstood and underestimated.

I don't want to idealise this, however, because it seems to me that at least part of this process operated through our expectations of the celebrity-as-commodity. It has occurred to me that the global mourning had a lot to do with our expectations as consumers, depending on the reliable provision of our favourite commodity: we fully expected that such a figure would continue to be available to play the part we allocated them in our lives. The continuing narrative of her life was indeed a commodity, offered to the public – along the lines Billig suggests – as a mode of public entertainment, as well as a location for the examination of what McGuigan calls 'the conduct of life' (2000: 111). The abrupt end of this narrative, its eruptive and unforeshadowed character, was simply shocking. No longer was the conduct of *her* life to be available to us in the same way. If Richard Johnson is right, though, that does seem to have been the raw material for the 'identity work' that was so fundamental to the cultural functions outlined in Johnson's essay: the construction of identity through cultural consumption.

CONSTRUCTING CULTURAL IDENTITIES

As we have seen, many discussions of shifts in the function of media over the last decade or so have noted the displacement of the media's information function in favour of the media's entertainment function. As we have also seen, not everyone applauds this, and so quite different conclusions can be drawn from it. The more pessimistic accounts argue that the public sphere is progressively impoverished by such a shift while the more optimistic ones argue that the media are now simply serving different purposes than they used to. Foremost among these different purposes is to play a primary role in the process through which individual subjects, communities, and nations construct their cultural identities. As we saw in the previous chapter, even those entertainments that are accused of being fundamental to the impoverishment of the public sphere – confessional talk shows, for instance – have also been discussed in terms of their positive participation in the construction of identity. Therefore, as the media play an ever more active role in the production of identity; as our consumption practices increasingly reflect choices that privilege the performance of identity; and as celebrity becomes an increasingly common component of media content; it is not surprising that celebrity should become one of the primary locations where the news and entertainment media participate in the construction of cultural identity.

Johnson emphasised that this process, in its relation to Diana, involved a continual play between identification and 'dis-identification'. This is not a simple matter of finding oneself a role model to emulate (or the reverse); it is more contingent and complicated than that. Furthermore, although Johnson uses the psychologistic term 'identity work' to describe how the audience might make use of the mass-mediated celebrity, it is necessary to stress the importance of the *playfulness* of so much of our consumption of celebrities. The construction of identity is at least as much play as work. Discovering, imagining and discarding identities is something that can be accomplished precisely without penalty through the practice of cultural consumption. That is its great value. Much of the user-generated content on the web, involving mash-ups, parodies, and so on, could be understood in this way. Similarly, when a women's magazine offers its readers advice on how to 'celebritise' their wardrobe, this offer is as likely to produce a playful and imaginative form of cultural consumption as it is to unproblematically support the interests of capital.

As we saw in Chapter 1, P. David Marshall (1997) articulates the discursive and ideological connection between the construction of cultural identities, individualism and consumer capitalism in order to argue that the continual reproduction of this connection is the overwhelming political function of celebrity. Without necessarily disagreeing with that diagnosis, it is helpful to also think about the consumption of celebrity at a slightly less structural level, as a highly contingent and negotiated social practice. At this level, celebrity is put to work productively by individuals choosing their identities with (apparently) the relative freedom that encourages qualified optimism. One doesn't have to be an optimist, though, to believe that while this practice entails some choice and contingency, it retains the possibility of more than a complacent politics. Consequently, Christine Gledhill can read the political function of 'stars' from a very different perspective to that taken in Marshall's work. 'Stardom enacts the power and material success of individual lives', says

Gledhill. Accordingly, they are 'implicated in the critique of individualism, consumerism and social stereotyping'. Rather than naturalising consumer capitalism then, 'they become an object of cultural politics' (Gledhill, 1991: xiv). A proper account of celebrity needs to acknowledge both possibilities, while recognising – as always – the larger frame around such a cultural politics that overdetermines its structural effects.

The significance of the dialectic between competing political possibilities has been recognised for a long time, of course. Richard Dyer's pioneering analyses (1979; 1986) of the social and cultural functions performed by the star have not only retained their relevance, but also remain among the most useful and succinct analyses of the cultural function of celebrities in general. In the theory of stardom Dyer works through in *Heavenly Bodies* (1986), he makes what is still a foundational observation: that 'stars articulate what it is to be a human being in contemporary society; that is, they express the particular notion we hold of the person, of the "individual"'. However, he goes on to stress that while stars perform this task, they 'do so complexly, variously – they are not straightforward affirmations of individualism'. On the contrary, he continues, 'they articulate both the promise and the difficulty that the notion of the individual presents for all of us who live by it' (1986: 8). The competing politics and the dual possibilities of such a practice are reflected in the complexity and variety of any particular star's 'performances, images and representations'. Indeed, due to the semiotic richness of the representational field, audiences require an underlying principle that will unify the wealth of available meanings that can be attached to the star. As Dyer points out, what gives the range of representations their coherence is the conviction – reinforced at the point of production and rearticulated in the process of consumption – that underlying all of this is an 'irreducible core' (ibid.: 10) that is the 'true identity' of the star as a person.

De Cordova offers an interesting sidelight on this conviction, alerted to it as a form of cultural pathology by the close temporal coincidence between the development of the cinema's star system and the development of psychoanalysis in the early decades of the twentieth century:

> Both [the star system and psychoanalysis] take identity (or even personality) as their object: both depend upon a model of surface and depth and search for the true identity beneath surface manifestations; both look to a private, familial identity to locate that truth, and both assume, furthermore, that that truth is, at its core, sexual. It is undoubtedly significant that these two systems of considering the question of identity should develop more or less simultaneously and share so many preoccupations, particularly if we admit that they have together ... so utterly dominated considerations of identity in this century. (1990: 144)

Cultural identity and celebrity have, it seems, a shared history and perhaps even a common origin. Dyer implies that our interest is directly related to the need to make sense of our experience of the current model of social production:

> We're fascinated by stars because they enact ways of making sense of the experience of being a person in a particular kind of social production (capitalism), with its particular organisation of life into public and private spheres. We love them because they represent how we think that experience is or how it would be lovely to feel that it is. Stars represent typical ways of behaving, feeling and thinking in contemporary society, ways that have been socially, culturally, historically constructed. (1986: 17)

We still need to know more, though, about the nature of the desire that this fascination expresses. This takes us into territory that is not particularly well developed in the available literature and so I'm going to leave this for another occasion.

At this point, I want to move away from the broad cultural construction of individual identities and look at something a little more specific. Over the 1990s, cultural studies' increased focus on the construction of individual or community cultural identities displaced an earlier concentration upon the workings of representation and ideology (Turner, 2003: Chapter 7). As a consequence, the relationship between celebrities and national identity – something that is important to Dyer's work both in *Stars* and *Heavenly Bodies* – receded from consideration to some extent. In many of the discussions of Princess Diana the focus was upon her global celebrity rather than the specificity of her dialogue with conceptions of British national identity. Johnson, however, spends quite some time on this issue in order to point out how fundamentally important was Diana's complicated, revisionist, relation to conventional versions of British-ness. 'Diana's Britain', as he describes it, was antithetical to the establishment: populist, to be sure, but committed to the importance of cultural difference and recognising the people as 'citizens' rather than as subjects of the Crown (Johnson, 1999: 35–6). Such a construction implies a degree of unity that is probably misleading, but the point to be made is that her celebrity – both in the UK and elsewhere – was built at least partly upon its challenge to complacent versions of British national identity.

Global media celebrities reflect the more complicated discursive connections between the global, the national and the local that operate now. Nonetheless, there is one category of celebrity where the consideration of their relation to national identity is unavoidable. Sports celebrities are still largely constructed through their connection to national identity. Frequently representing the nation formally (in the national team, for instance), their professional careers depend upon how successfully they perform. In most cases this will mean the quality of their sporting performances, but there are other areas of performance that matter too (sportsmanship on the field, their behaviour when celebrating in the bar after the game, their conduct while sharing an airliner with the public and so on). As 'ambassadors' for their country or for the game they play, standards of appropriate behaviour will apply far more stringently for a high profile member of the English soccer team, say, than for a Hollywood movie star. Hence, English foot-baller Wayne Rooney can expect less tolerance from his fans and from game administrators than Leonardo DiCaprio can expect from his fans and from the industry that employs him. The media, furthermore, are likely to take a more censorious and moralistic line than the fans or the industry.

Generally, the process of identity formation involved in the consumption of celebrity does not involve anything as crude as role-modelling, but there are grounds for qualifying this observation in the case of the sports star. Perhaps as a legacy of high-minded ideals deriving from late nineteenth-century constructions of sporting competitions as the ideal location for the display of masculine heroism, it is common for sports stars to be reminded of their responsibilities as role models for their fans. This is not something that tends to be required of celebrities from other industries (we don't ask this of Ozzy Osbourne, for instance, or Robert Downey Jnr). It should be admitted, though, that the expectation that sports stars should serve such a function seems more firmly grounded in the attitudes of sports administrators and the sports media, than in those of sports fans. Certainly, as Whannel says in *Media Sports Stars*, 'there is little convincing evidence that the relation between the young audience and stars in the public eye is as simple as the "role model" concept implies' (2002: 7). Nor is there is any reason to suppose that sports fans are any less aware of the constructed nature of the sports celebrity's mediated image than other kinds of fan. Nonetheless, once a sports star is seen to have 'let the fans down' (or in many cases, let the *country* down[3]) they can expect a thorough rebuke from the media, and to have this taken up in the taunts from the crowd when they step on to the field. Their performance as exemplary figures does affect the management of their careers and the discourses that surround and motivate their consumption. Therefore, it doesn't matter so much if sports stars actually *do* function as role models. What is more important is the fact that they are characteristically discussed in the media and in public discourse generally as if they do so and that their performance in this capacity is of public, and even national, concern (ibid.: 7).

The difficulty this presents to the sports celebrity is exacerbated by the fact that sport, with its 'ethical structure of fair play, its roots in Corinthian idealism and its separateness from the contestations of the political sphere, appeals to the moral entrepreneurs' (Whannel, 2002: 7). The careers of sports stars are especially vulnerable to the mass-mediated cycle of 'celebration, transgression, punishment and redemption' that Garry Whannel documents in his account of the career of British footballer Paul Gascoigne (ibid.: Chapter 11). The playing out of this cycle – through tabloid revelations, paparazzi shots, interviews with aggrieved friends, spouses or team-mates, moralistic commentary pieces, contrite confessions, and even comments from politicians – is offered to the public as an entertainment, with the sports star concerned a more or less powerless participant. The content of such cycles is not arbitrary, of course. Whannel's book examines how social anxieties about morality, about social behaviour and about the performance of masculinity, are played out through representations of and debate about the conduct and performance of sports stars. Unlike their counterparts in the entertainment industries, the sports star (particularly the male sports star[4]) is asked to personify what signifies as the heroic in this society at this time. Their efforts to meet this request help to satisfy the media's thirst for scrutinising the spectacle of the performance of celebrity. Focusing overwhelmingly on how men should behave, sports celebrity plays its part in facilitating what McGuigan described earlier as the 'popular deliberation on the conduct of life'. Ironically, partly as a result of the enthusiasm of the moral entrepreneurs and the editorial preferences of the tabloids, such deliberation largely occurs in relation to the transgression of the accepted norms of conduct, not their confirmation or inscription. Typically, it is the sports stars' indiscretions in their private lives (think, Tiger Woods) that will expose them to criticism and not their performance as sports-persons (although Lance Armstrong managed to disappoint in such a comprehensive manner that it involved both his public and his private life).

Notwithstanding such specificities, there are many ways in which the consumption of the sports hero repeats the patterns we have seen in relation to film stars, television personalities and other celebrities from the media and entertainment industries. The desire for the authentic – to reach the core of the personality, to find out what 'they are really like' – is as fundamental to the sports fan as to the film fan. The sports fan is as much at the mercy of the production industry, too, in the choices available to them for consumption in the first place. Fundamental, in fact, is what Whannel calls 'the paradox of productive consumption and consumptive production': that is, we are both the producer and consumer of our own pleasures, but we are not in control of their supply. Or as he puts it in a slightly more elaborated way: 'football fans, music lovers and other enthusiasts live out an intense and pleasurable relation to the object of their passion, and also, *at the same time*, recognise it as commodified, transformed and out of their reach' (2002: 201).

How such consumption actually operates in various contexts, the complicated playing out of the cultural function of celebrity, is what I want to discuss in the following chapter. What I have been examining in this chapter is a particularly productive form of consumption – the 'identity work' that celebrity facilitates. As we have seen, celebrity is as likely to produce derision and resentment as admiration, so there are other kinds of processing which occur that are much less productive. Some of these will be dealt with in Chapter 6. However, since so much of this chapter has located the cultural function of celebrity within the context of the consumption of media representations, it is important to raise another aspect of this process before concluding. One of the ways through which media representations are integrated into our everyday lives is via talk – gossip. (Or, at least, it is usually called gossip when it involves women, but just talk when it involves men.) Gossip is a way of sharing social judgements and of processing social behaviour, and this is true whether it involves people we know directly or people we know solely through their media presence. Gossip is also one of the fundamental processes employed as a means of social and cultural identity formation.

Research suggests that the purpose of gossip about celebrities is not to elevate or idealise them as exemplary individuals. The choice of figures about whom gossip will be exchanged is as likely to include those regarded with resentment or derision as those regarded as heroic. Significantly, however, gossip seems to serve an assimilating and normalising function, providing a means of integrating the celebrity and the stories about them into one's everyday life. Joke Hermes' work on media audiences (1999) led her to observe that her respondents' 'interest in the details of celebrities' lives would, among other things, seems to be a means of bringing them down to the level of ordinary human beings and to imagine them as part of their extended families'.[5] This, Hermes continued, is how social existence in western societies worked: 'seeing media figures as real and as part of our everyday cultural and emotional experience is part and parcel of how media texts come to have meaning' (1999: 71). It is easy to underestimate the importance of this kind of meaning making and to therefore assume it is not going on at all. In the case of Diana, the focus upon what was assumed to be the media's manipulation of this process prevented the acknowledgment of the cultural function of the central relationship involved. In the following chapter, I want to talk a little more about gossip as well as some other modes of consumption to which celebrity is now available.

NOTES

1 In Australia, where I was when Diana died, this meant that free-to-air networks simply switched to live feeds from the global cable networks such as CNN and BBC World, and ran them for hours uninterrupted by advertisements.

2 Of course, it is important to remember that she wasn't really. She was an aristocrat, the daughter of an earl, and entitled to call herself Lady Diana. Frances Bonner has made the point to me in her comments on this chapter that it is important to recognise that the construction of her as a commoner was the consequence of a lot of representational work – and in particular an excessive emphasis on her job (she was an aide in a pre-school) and her sharing a flat – just like the common people.

3 According to Whannel, in his treatment of the career of British footballer Paul Gascoigne, his 'major crime' was not letting down his wife, his children, or himself, but rather 'letting down his country' (2002: 145).

4 As Whannel points out in his preface, 'it is not simply that interest in sport is far more common among men, and hostility to sport more common among women, but rather that the very practices of sport are still distinctly bound up with the production of masculinities' (2002: ix). Such a situation makes it doubly difficult for women to achieve the level of national prominence offered to men. When the women also represent a marginalised group – as does Australian indigenous athlete Cathy Freeman, for instance – then the identity work they enable is both challenging and substantial and worth close analysis in its own right (see Hartley, 2008).

5 Rojek offers another version of this formulation: 'celebrity culture is one of the most important mechanisms for mobilizing abstract desire' because it embodies desire in an 'animate object' – it 'humanizes' desire (2001: 189).

6   Consuming Celebrity

We may not like the same celebrities, we may not like any of them at all, but it is the existence of a population of celebrities, about whom to disagree, that makes it possible to constitute a sense of belonging. Through celebrating (or deriding) celebrities it is possible to belong to something beyond the particular culture with which each of us might identify. (Wark, 1999: 33)

CELEBRITY WATCHERS

Part of the task for Chapter 5 was to find a way of explaining, rather than dismissing, the public affection for Diana. As a consequence of this focus, the emphasis was necessarily upon the productive consumption of celebrity – and specifically its participation in the process of identity formation. While that is certainly a major aspect of the cultural function of celebrity, and the Diana example provides a rich location to examine this aspect, it is not the only one. Nor is it the case that celebrity is always consumed in ways that are productive or progressive. As I have noted repeatedly throughout this book, celebrity – as a discourse, as a commodity, as a spectacle – is marked by contradictions, ambiguities and ambivalences. There are many forms and sites of consumption: from attending writers' festivals to visiting celebrity porn sites on the internet. The mode of engagement in the various forms and sites can vary dramatically. Where engaging with particular celebrities may produce experiences as intense and reflective as those outlined in Richard Johnson's essay discussed in the previous chapter, other forms of engagement may seem entirely superficial, almost random, in their occurrence. Once we start to talk about specifics, it becomes clear that the consumption of celebrity is highly individualised and requires careful contextualisation. Fans, readers and viewers will have their own menu of personalities and attributes in which they will maintain an interest – and their own reasons for doing so.[1] It is important to recognise that regarding the consumption of celebrity as explicable through one set of principles, as serving one set of politics, or as operating through one modality, is to misunderstand the cultural processes in play (Turner et al., 2000: 178).

In this chapter, then, I want to discuss the wider variety of consumption practices through which the cultural function of celebrity is performed. A first point of variation acknowledges the different levels of media literacy evident in consumers' responses to the celebrity industry. It is possible to say that some sections of the audience appear to be quite gullible about the 'truth' of what they see, hear or read; whereas others seem to be extremely well informed about the industry processes and therefore about the constructed-ness of what they see, hear or read. However, all the evidence suggests that one does not have to believe that what one reads about a celebrity is true in order to happily pursue the consumption of celebrity.

This leads us to a more fundamental set of variations, which have to do with the shifting nature of the consumer-commodity relation itself. Joshua Gamson developed a typology that mapped the levels and characteristics of the audience's engagement with the consumption of celebrity. He conducted focus groups with 'celebrity watchers' as part of his *Claims to Fame* project.[2] He was interested, initially, in whether it made a difference for the production of celebrity to be invisible and whether knowledge of the operation of the publicity industry had an effect on the celebrity watchers' engagement. He also tested audiences' assumptions about how 'real' or 'true' they thought stories about celebrities might be and whether such considerations were important to the pleasures intrinsic to consuming celebrity. Gamson categorised the outcomes of the focus group discussions in a typology that distinguished five 'audience types'. The group he called 'the traditional' audience regarded the celebrity text (that is, the representations of celebrity they encountered in their media use) as realistic and celebrity stories as arising naturally through the news media rather than generated through promotions or publicity strategies. They demonstrated low levels of awareness of the production process. As Gamson puts it, they were 'ignorant' of the 'story's production, passive in encountering it, and powerless in the face of its ideas and effects' (1994: 147). Gamson describes the category's interaction with celebrity as involving 'modelling, fantasy and identification' (ibid.: 146).

The second category of audience type was the 'second-order traditional', where a little more interpretation occurred, and the attribution of realism was more qualified:

> 'Inside stories' of the 'real lives' of celebrities and opportunities to see them as 'themselves' may be mobilized to anchor truth and merit and weed out impostors. [These] audiences see a more complex narrative in which publicity mechanisms play a part but do not pose an obstacle to [holding the celebrities in high] esteem. (ibid.: 147)

This audience type believed in the 'deserving celebrity', as well as in their own capacity to discern 'authenticity' by interpreting the media representations. They too were involved in modelling, fantasy and identification with the media figures, according to Gamson, but in a more negotiated manner.

The third audience type was marked by their reading of the celebrity stories as more or less fictional, artificially created and demanding evaluation and interpretation. These, the 'postmodernist' audience type, 'know about celebrity manufacture and seek out its evidence and its details, rejecting or ignoring the story of the naturally rising[3] celebrity as naive and false'. Far from being put off by this, however, the postmodernist audience type is actively interested in 'the techniques of artifice in and of themselves' (ibid.: 147).

The fourth and fifth types are defined as, respectively, 'Game player: gossiper' and 'Game player: detective'. These types regard the content of the stories as semi-fictional, they aren't bothered too much about where the stories come from or if they reveal the 'truth' about the celebrity concerned, and their awareness of the production process is 'medium to high' (ibid.: 146). What distinguishes these audience types is their making use of celebrity material for play, for experimentation, as fodder for their own cultural activities. Gamson suggests that they do not invest in celebrity as a system at all, even though their behaviour as consumers may actually look like that of fans: 'their involvement may be based on pleasures that simply bypass the questions of [the deserved nature of] claims to fame or that even make use of both the stories and the ambiguity they together create' (ibid.: 147). Celebrity production is, for the 'detective', a giant discursive playground and for 'the gossiper' a rich social resource. As Gamson puts it, these audiences 'use celebrities not as models or fantasies but as opportunities' (ibid.: 147).

Gamson's research suggests that the celebrity system survives precisely because it can sustain such a broad spectrum of modes of consumption. Certainly, it is interesting to note how fortuitous it is that the variations are mutually supportive. On the evidence Gamson provides, those who believe most in the truth of celebrity representation are also those who know least about the processes of production; however, those who know most about the processes of production have no interest in establishing the authenticity of the celebrities themselves.

This typology is useful in that it provides us with a description of modes of engagement and of consumption practices. However, I would suggest that contemporary consumption practices no longer necessarily fall neatly into the categories that Gamson outlines. Indeed, it is likely that any one individual consumer might adopt the position of a number of these audience types in their specific dealings with celebrity from time to time. Furthermore, the contemporary pervasiveness and cultural mobility of celebrity would suggest that the consumption strategies employed by media audiences have become increasingly sophisticated and contingent. For evidence of this I would point to the media formats currently dominating industry developments, reality TV game-shows such as *The Bachelor* (currently in its seventeenth season), for instance, where it is precisely the modalities of the constructed and the real that generate the 'playing field' of the game for the audience. Not to be interested in the negotiation of these modalities would be to miss much of the point of the game.

As a result, one might suggest, it is Gamson's 'game player' that is now the dominant form of audience type inscribed into these mainstream media formats. Annette Hill's discussion of *Big Brother* implicitly supports such a possibility. She describes a mode of watching which suggests that quite subtle and highly contingent interpretative and identificatory strategies are put into play. Audiences, she argues, watch *Big Brother* as a 'gamedoc' (that is, as a hybrid game-show and documentary) while still pursuing what Hill regards as a typical goal of the consumption of celebrity material – sorting out the authentic from the constructed and finding out what the contestants are 'really like' (the position of Gamson's 'traditionals'):

> Viewers' strategies for watching factual TV are, in my opinion, several moves ahead of the game. If part of the attraction of watching *Big Brother* is to look for a moment of authenticity in relation to selfhood, then audiences are responding to the hybrid of performance and reality that has come to characterize much factual entertainment. The 'game' is to find the 'truth' in the spectacle/performance environment. (Hill, 2002: 337)

As I say, this is a sophisticated interpretative activity, but it does not strike me as in any way atypical of contemporary media consumption; indeed, it is much the kind of thing we would expect to find in the consumption of gossip magazines, as well as constituting what Marwick and boyd (2011) highlight as one of the key pleasures of using Twitter. This is the behaviour of the fan, in fact, rather than that of the casual consumer. It reflects the extent to which the fan's mode of consumption has moved from 'the cult' to the mainstream as increased levels of personalisation and interactivity have become routine components of the processes of consumption in the digital era, and as the fan has become increasingly embedded in what Hills (2002: 177) calls the 'commodity-text' of the celebrity through their contributions to the construction of the celebrity's online persona.

Perhaps this is to slightly privilege the knowing playfulness of celebrity consumption – a tendency that is visible in Gamson's book as well as in aspects of Joke Hermes' work. This tendency does have its strategic uses, though, in this context. It helps to highlight what we might describe as the *lack* of emotional investment that can accompany so much of the consumption of celebrity – counteracting those media panics about people identifying with their favourite celebrity to the point where it interferes with their daily lives and personal relations.[4] One of the more newsworthy academic takes on celebrity has been McCutcheon et al's (2002, 2004) studies of what they describe as 'celebrity worship' – a phrase that describes an adulatory mode of celebrity consumption as if it was the dominant or even the only modality in play in order to raise social concerns about the pathologies it engenders. To describe the function of celebrity solely in these terms leaves out a great deal of the pleasures that the consumption of celebrity can generate. In his discussion of fans' participation in the popular website TelevisionWithoutPity.com, Mark Andrejevic captures the contradictory nature of this participation. Priding itself on its 'snarkastic' treatment of its favourite television programmes, often generating 'sarcastic and savagely funny recaps of selected shows', the site nonetheless is marked by a 'combination of enthusiasm and criticism' as a result of its hosting, in effect, 'two, not entirely distinct, types of forums: those populated by serious fans who admire the show and those devoted to viewers who love to mock the show being discussed' (2008: 31). The snarky, cynical pleasures of ridicule, parody and derision that make TelevisionWithoutPity so attractive also pepper the celebrity blogosphere in general.

In addition, and often right alongside this modality, however, there are also the more creative and playful forms of user-generated content that use celebrity as the raw material for comic invention. The circulation of the Sad Keanu meme,[5] for instance, is simply 'good clean fun', as Keanu Reeves described it to an interviewer on BBC breakfast TV in 2011. A paparazzi shot of a pensive Keanu Reeves sitting on a park bench eating a sandwich in New York City is photoshopped in all kinds of ways: his image is perched on Mitt Romney's shoulder, sat in the 'empty chair' addressed by Clint Eastwood at the Republican convention, and glumly accompanying a bunch of thrill-seekers on a rollercoaster ride. The appropriation of Keanu's image has little to do with 'celebrity worship', but much to do with the availability and accessibility of that image, and its baggage of meanings, for comic invention and play.

This tendency, then, is helpful in arguing against the pathologisation of consumption that Joli Jenson criticised in Richard Schickel (see Chapter 5). It should not be sold short as simply another instance of cultural populism. There is plenty of evidence that, for some, 'play' is an accurate description of their dominant mode of engagement with celebrity. Gamson focuses at some length on groups of celebrity watchers who see the whole thing as a game. He notes that issues of truth and reality, authenticity and inauthenticity, do not present as issues to be resolved but as territories for play. The contemporary formats used for celebrity gossip enable this: the 'pleasurable freedom of celebrity gossip', he says, is built 'precisely on its freedom from but resemblance to truth' (1994: 177). The attraction of this material does not depend on whether or not it is true; the pleasure is in the social exchange it facilitates:

> Celebrities are like neighbours whom nearly everyone knows, in nearly every social setting, and 'stuff' about them is easier to find and share than information about your friends and colleagues. More important, celebrity gossip is a much *freer* realm, much more game-like than acquaintance gossip: there are no repercussions and there is no accountability. (1994: 176)

Gamson's discussion here moves from classifying celebrity watchers so as to understand and differentiate their varying modes of engagement to focusing upon some of the practices through which these engagements are played out. Prominent among these is gossip and in the next section of this chapter I want to focus a little more closely upon the social functions performed by celebrity gossip.

GOSSIP: THE EXTENDED FAMILY, MELODRAMA AND REVENGE

> The celebrities are disposable. The gossip is priceless.
>
> (Masthead motto, Oh No They Didn't! celebrity gossip website.)

Already in this book, I have noted the social function of gossip – its role in generating social networks, evaluating behaviour, establishing community norms and so on. I have dealt with the issue of the apparently 'para-social' nature of the exchanges described in the previous chapter. In this section, I want to examine the role of gossip as a consumption practice a little further. My starting point is Lynn Spigel's discussion of what I would regard as a related phenomenon: the imbrication of the television family sitcom into suburban everyday life in America during the 1950s. Lynn Spigel's book, *Welcome to the Dreamhouse* (2001), examines the early development of the relation between the American television audience and the television celebrity – a relation she locates in postwar suburbia. Focusing upon the early family television sitcoms, many of which had migrated to television from radio (*The Adventures of Ozzie and Harriet, I Love Lucy, The George Burns and Gracie Allen Show*, for example), Spigel suggests that these shows helped to blur the lines 'between electrical and real space. Television families were typically presented as "real families" who just happened to live their lives on TV' (2001: 44). She points out that this applied to television families who were also real-life families, the Nelsons and the Ball-Arnaz's for instance, but also to those who were not – such as the actors in *The Danny Thomas Show*. Spigel suggests that one of the functions of these television families was that they helped mediate the alienation produced by the American 'flight to the suburbs':

> They helped ease what must have been for many Americans a painful transition from the city to the suburb. But more than simply supplying a tonic for displaced suburbanites, television promised something better: it promised a mode of spectator pleasure premised on the sense of an illusory – rather than a real – community of friends. It held out a new possibility for being alone in the home, away from the troublesome busy-body neighbours in the next house. But it also maintained ideals of community togetherness and social interconnection by placing the community *at a fictional distance*. Television allowed people to enter into an imaginary social life, one that was shared not in the neighbourhood networks of bridge clubs and mahjong gatherings but on the national networks of CBS, NBC and ABC. (Spigel, 2001: 45)

Consequently, Spigel goes on to suggest that television at the time promised 'a new kind of social experience, one that replicates the logic of real friendship ... but that transforms it into an imaginary social relationship shared between the home audience and the television image' (ibid.: 46). Far from this being unreal (and here, her account is reminiscent of the production of royal majesty for Billig's family respondents [1992]), the ability of television to create a sense of 'being there' produced a kind of *hyperrealism* (ibid.: 46). It is as if the televisual belonged to a higher order of reality rather than a field of representations.

Although this is applied to a media format we have not really dealt with at all in this book, what is being described is familiar to us. It could easily be translated into arguments about the role of celebrity gossip. Indeed, there are strong similarities between Spigel's account above, and that provided by Neal Gabler as he describes the appeal – and the social function – of the genre of gossip journalism that Walter Winchell invented:

> Sociologist Louis Wirth had distinguished between the concept of *community*, where individuals knew one another and were bound by ties of kinship and neighbourhood, and the concept of *society*, where secondary relationships increasingly supplanted primary ones. As the twenties transformed America from a community into a society, gossip seemed to provide one of the lost ingredients of the former for the latter: a common frame of reference. In gossip everyone was treated as a known quantity; otherwise the gossip was meaningless. In gossip one could create a national 'backyard fence' over which all Americans could chat. (Gabler, 1995: 80–1)

Such angles of analysis produce the idea that our interaction with these media figures, and our conversations about them, can be understood in terms of their participation in the construction of community. Notwithstanding gossip's perjorative associations in common usage, there is substantial support for Hermes' view that what she calls 'serious gossip' can 'serve to enlarge the reader's private world, and to create moral community' (1995: 120).

Hermes' comments emanate from a research project during which she interviewed readers of women's celebrity gossip magazines in the Netherlands. Her research recognised the pleasurable construction of 'an imaginary social life', as Spigel would put it. The way this imaginary social life works, Hermes argues, can be understood by focusing upon the constitutive discourses through which conversations about celebrity operate. One of the two primary 'repertoires' of discourse about celebrity she distinguishes through her research is what she describes as the 'extended family' repertoire. The extended family repertoire 'draws a wide circle of people into a person's private life by discussing them intimately', extending the social and moral community in which we live: it offers 'the pleasure of extending your family by including the stars' (ibid.: 124):

> On an imaginary level it helps readers to live in a larger world than in real life – a world that is governed by emotional ties, that may be shaken by divorces and so on, but that is never seriously threatened. Sociological realities such as high divorce rates, broken families, children who leave home hardly ever to be seen again, are temporarily softened. The world of gossip is like the world of soap opera: whatever happens, they do not fall apart. (Hermes, 1999: 80)[6]

The celebrity is integrated into everyday life as a family member would be, but without the network of responsibility and obligation such a relation normally involves. This, in conjunction with the potential for play discussed in the previous section, helps to explain the productiveness and attraction of celebrity gossip.

While celebrity gossip offers a way of imaginatively enriching one's community, it also domesticates desire, producing a levelling effect that counteracts the asymmetry of media-audience power relations in other contexts. In outlining the politics of the 'Game player: gossip' audience type, Gamson emphasises this potential:

> [This audience type] refuses the text's conventional integration of the production system into the story line of earned prestige, usually acknowledging artifice and manipulation with indifference. Gossip refuses, in essence, the prestige and admiration offered by the text, the vertical relationship offered between celebrity and watcher, opting instead for a system of collective evaluation and horizontal relationships between gossipers. (1994: 177–8)

Skeggs and Wood's (2012) research among audiences of makeover reality TV programmes found a similar process was in play, as audiences engaged in what Skeggs and Wood call 'tournaments of value' in their interpretation of what they saw. The conversations through which the depicted behaviour was assessed and evaluated served to re-integrate the performances on screen with the structures of the audiences' daily lives. Gamson is not alone in regarding gossip of this kind as a form of social and cultural empowerment. Neal Gabler, in his biography of Walter Winchell, attributes to the gossip columnist a similar view:

> Having grown up in poverty himself, attention-starved, and nursing deep resentments against his social betters, [Winchell] understood that gossip, far beyond its basic attraction as journalistic voyeurism, was a weapon of empowerment for the reader and listener. Invading the lives of the famous and revealing their secrets brought them to heel. It humanized them, and in humanizing them demonstrated that they were not better than we and in many cases worse. (1995: xiii)

The second 'repertoire' of celebrity discourse that Joke Hermes outlines is the repertoire of melodrama. This repertoire creates community in a very different manner, and is far more ambivalent and complex:

> The repertoire of melodrama can be recognised in references to misery, drama and by its sentimentalism and sensationalism, but also by its moral undertone. Life in the repertoire of melodrama becomes grotesquely magnified. In the vale of tears that it is, celebrities play crucial and highly stereotyped roles, reminiscent of folk and oral culture. (1999: 80)

This repertoire comes into play when 'readers are indignant, when they are shocked or deeply moved, and wish to evaluate explicitly what they have heard' (Hermes, 1995: 131). Celebrities become the locations for the discussion and evaluation of the dramatic happenings of everyday life: divorces, deaths, disappointments in career and so on. The sensationalism of much of the representation of celebrity lives seems to be a key component of its melodramatic function, and the emotions it generates are not necessarily generous or benign. Indeed, Hermes relates that some of her respondents gave her examples of how 'the misery of others made them feel better about their own lives', or helped them deal with their own frustrations or sorrow (1999: 80).

This is a mode of consumption that feeds off the melodramatic imagination of the consumer, on the one hand, and a store of socially grounded resentment, on the other:

> However, at the heart of the repertoire of melodrama, there is also a deep sense that the world is unjust, which points to a more collective sense of social inequality. To enjoy it when things are going badly for 'rich and

famous people' (as one of my readers put it) is a way of imagining cosmic (rather than political) justice taking its toll. Commiseration and indignation are equal ingredients of the pleasure of reading gossip magazines. (ibid.: 81)

Again, Neal Gabler employs a similar formulation in his discussion of the politics of Walter Winchell's columns. Here, too, the gossip column sets things right, serving the interests of 'justice in a corrupt world'. Winchell's invention is described as an act of defiance that empowered his readers to wreak vengeance through their appropriation of the meanings generated by the images of the rich, the powerful, the famous and the privileged (1995: 81). Similarly, Ian Connell insisted in 1992 that the tabloid treatment of celebrity was not about offering figures for admiration but was instead a means of mounting a 'populist challenge on privilege': 'they give voice to and vent pent-up frustration and indignation at the excesses of those who have come from recognisably ordinary backgrounds and have "made it" in understandable ways' (1992: 74). He points out, though, that this frustration and indignation can be quite fun to express – or as he puts it, 'powerfully and pleasurably engaging'. Therefore, it does not constitute a protest at the social and media structures that produce these people. It is more specific than that; people are not, he suggests, 'against privileges being granted, merely angry that they have been granted to the wrong people – to "them" and not to "us"' (1992: 82). So the details matter. As a result, the decision about which people to resent is one for highly elaborated judgements that are made in conjunction with others: socially, discursively, and often pleasurably, in conversation.

Hermes stresses, though, that both these repertoires of celebrity discourse are motivated by 'a wish for and a forging of community, a quality that', she argues, 'is inherent in all gossip' (1995: 128). In making this point, Hermes is at pains to challenge the commonsense assumption that gossip about celebrities is about evaluating and emulating role models.[7] 'Going by the two repertoires I found', she says, 'reading gossip magazines revolves not around fantasies of perfect selves but around fantasies of belonging: to an extended family or a moral community' (ibid.: 132).

Couldry's view, that the pursuit of celebrity constitutes a bid to enter the social centre, may be consonant with this. There are also reminders of this motivation in the analysis that Gamson provides of his crowd of celebrity watchers outside the Academy Awards in Los Angeles. Gamson stands in the bleachers with the crowd beside the red carpet awaiting the arrival of the stars and notes the celebrity watchers' behaviour towards the objects of their attention. One of the details he picks up is the importance of receiving acknowledgment from the celebrities parading past. It does not matter, interestingly, which celebrity provides the wave of acknowledgment; any form of recognition from anyone of this status is regarded as a kind of validation for the celebrity watcher. They have, albeit briefly, gained access to the centre of social power:

> The celebrities are treated, if not as a traditional power elite, as an elite with the power to anoint, however briefly. In a formal democracy, personal distinction, self-importance, glory and honour are ideologically problematic and hard to achieve. Celebrities as an elite mediate this problem: they have been legitimated by popularity, distinguished by the fact that millions of eyes have dwelled on them, by the glamour of envy. (Gamson, 1994: 132)

It is important to acknowledge the contradictions underlying what I have been saying about the social function of gossip in this context. Just as we have seen in relation to other concepts dealt with in this book, the celebrity is processed through gossip as a spectacular commodity – interesting and entertaining in their own right. However, they are also strenuously appropriated to the social tasks conventionally attributed to gossip: sharing judgements, values and norms through the conversation about individuals 'known' to all participants. The construction of community through gossip is a multi-faceted activity: generating expressions of admiration, class-envy, revenge, or simply circulating rumours that are possibly untrue but which are happily shared nonetheless.

Perhaps, the great value of Hermes' and Gamson's work is not so much that it provides us with an explanation of the function of celebrity in the particular instances they consider, although it certainly does this well, but that it demonstrates celebrity's social, cultural and political contingency. As with popular culture in general, it is necessary to remember that this is a variously determined field of cultural relations, not a set of invariate structures, and the attempt to read off its political function or the cultural meanings it appears to privilege has to be contextualised within particular historical conjunctures. So far, there are not many accounts of the consumption of celebrity that have set out to do this. In the following section, I want to talk briefly about one example.

HISTORIES OF CONSUMPTION: STAR GAZING

> What do you think a celebrity is? It's someone sent to us as a gift, to bring us joy. (1980s' celebrity Angelyne, quoted in Gamson, 1994: 1)

There are historicised studies of individual stars, or the celebrity case study, of course. Dyer's *Heavenly Bodies* (1986) is a key model, while Marshall's studies of Oprah Winfrey and New Kids on the Block (1997) and Cashmore's study of David Beckham (2003) are among the relatively few dealing with celebrities other than film stars. Film studies remains the most well-developed area for this kind of work, with the social history of the audience becoming an increasingly important part of its historiography. Miriam Hansen's (1991) work on the audiences for silent film has been particularly influential in its demonstration of how one might deal with such phenomena at an historical distance. In her case, of course, she did not have direct access to fans for their testimony and so was unable to build on the possibilities developed by television audience studies from the 1980s. (I have in mind here the models provided by Dorothy Hobson [1982], Ien Ang [1985] and David Morley [1986]). However, in similar ways to the approach undertaken in Ien Ang's *Watching Dallas* (1985), Jackie Stacey's book, *Star Gazing* (1994), is able to make direct contact with film audiences and to learn from her respondents' letters as they talk about their experiences.

Despite its title, Stacey's book is not so much about stars as about their audiences. She deals with the American female cinema stars of the 1940s and 1950s and their British fans at the time. *Star Gazing* focuses on female fans' memories and associations with stars in order to understand the specific appeal of the stars themselves: it examines the uses to which they were put, the pleasures they provided, and how they were integrated into the audiences' everyday lives. At times, the focus is on other things than celebrity: Stacey describes the book as a study of 'white British women's fantasies about glamour, about Americanness and about themselves' (1994: 17). The stars emerge as a useful means of providing analytic access to contemporary discourses about a range of other topics. The dramatic shift in British popular culture as it modernises and Americanises after the war, and the popular receptiveness to the discourses of consumerism, are both well caught in this account of women's experiences.

Among the particular benefits of Stacey's study is a considered and nuanced analysis of the idea that cinema offered a form of escapism for its audiences. She provides us with a revised and renovated conception of escapism that rejects the commonsense assumption that it might constitute an irresponsible disregard for contemporary realities. Indeed, as Stacey puts it, she has 'reversed' escapism's negative connotations as a starting point for taking its pleasures seriously:

> The memories I have analysed have highlighted the many levels at which escapism provided pleasures for female spectators: material, sensuous, emotional as well as psychic. For example, the cinema interiors provided a utopian space and numerous sensuous luxuries; the feelings of being in an audience offered a sense of belonging and togetherness; and the stars were enjoyed as

utopian transcendent fantasies. Thus, it was not simply the visual pleasures of film texts that operated, but rather a whole range of appeals which encouraged the feelings of complete absorption into another world. (Stacey, 1994: 122–3)

Given the nature of the world from which these women sought release – wartime and immediate postwar Britain – it is not hard to see why such pleasures would be eagerly accepted.

Stacey's interrogation of her respondents' accounts demonstrates how useful the cinema was in terms of providing women with discourses through which they might construct their own identities; how pleasurable the cinema was as a social space for women; and how historically specific the accounts of female spectatorship need to be if they are to help us understand the relations between women audiences and women on the screen. Notably, the relations described are not static. Over the course of the book, Stacey highlights a 'significant shift in the cinematic mode of perception for female spectators in Britain at this time'. During the Second World War and the immediate postwar period, she argues, Hollywood stars were represented through 'discourses of difference which maximise[d] the distance between the spectator and the star at a number of symbolic levels':

> Not only is this difference structured through the notion of Hollywood glamour as an impossible ideal in the austere Britain of the 1940s, but also 'Americanness' at this time continues to hold the fascination of otherness. Economic and geographical distance from the stars thus combine in the cultural recognition of their difference from spectators. Thus 'distance' represents the symbolic spatial location of the female spectator in relation to Hollywood stars in wartime and postwar Britain. (Stacey, 1994: 234)

Stars were fantasy figures during this period, offering impossible images of wealth and glamour to their fans. Glamour becomes quite a key term, used to differentiate between the British and American construction of femininity in the cinema; as a result of the glamour factor, 'stars' came from Hollywood while 'actors' came from the British cinema (ibid.: 113). The difference in potential was dramatically reflected at the most basic levels of consumption in Britain at the time. Not only were there few opportunities for British women to reproduce the glamour they saw on the screen, there were also few opportunities to buy *any* clothes at all (ibid.: 114).

However, as Britain emerges from this period and as consumerism expands across the society over the mid to late 1950s, the symbolic and material distance between Hollywood and the British fans diminishes. The opportunity of consuming commodities like those identified with the Hollywood stars increased fans' symbolic and imaginative proximity to those stars, as well as the practical possibilities of their being in some way like them through commodity consumption. Concurrent with this was the increasing 'Americanisation' of British popular culture during the 1950s and the gradual blurring of the sharp geographical and cultural differences that had shaped so much of British cultural life during the previous decade. As a result of such shifts, Stacey's respondents record a significant shift in the positioning of Hollywood stars:

> Spectators' memories of stars suggest an increasingly interactive relationship between self-image and star ideals with the opening up of multiple possibilities of becoming more like the screen ideal through the purchase of commodities associated with particular stars. Mimetic self-transformations become an imaginable possibility through consumption – be it the suits or blonde hair of Marilyn Monroe, or the styles, fabrics and colours associated with Doris Day. These masquerades of stardom-femininity are embodiments of desirable qualities which bring the desirable object closer to the self. (1994: 236)

Interestingly this offers a slightly different and perhaps more nuanced reading of the discursive and corporate connections between the growth of consumer capitalism and Hollywood than we find in Marshall (1997), for instance, or De Cordova (1990). The focus on the individual needs of the consumer retrieves the productive cultural – and not just the economic – possibilities involved in the commodity consumption generated by the Hollywood star.

From one point of view this might not be seen as serving women's interests particularly well, in that the objectification of the female body is one of its effects. However, Stacey is characteristically alert to the nuanced complexity of such relations, even when they appear to be thoroughly commodified. She argues that 'the consumption practices of the female spectator are not entirely recuperable by patriarchal culture in this way':

> Paradoxically, whilst commodity consumption for female spectators in mid to late 1950s Britain concerns producing oneself as a desirable object, it also offers an escape from what is perceived as the drudgery of domesticity and motherhood which increasingly comes to define femininity at this time. (Stacey, 1994: 237–8)

Nevertheless, Stacey describes a shift in perception during which the Hollywood star is no longer viewed as if they come from another planet, to a point where they might be understood as a possible ideal, against which one's own body and one's own identity are constructed. What this shift sets in train is an enhanced process of cultural consumption of consumer goods, and the expansion of the facilities for this process is part of the history of the imagined relation between Hollywood stars and their British audiences:

> My argument ... is not based on an assumption that all female spectators at this time had an unlimited facility to purchase any number of the outfits they had seen and desired on the Hollywood screen. Indeed such a luxury remains the privilege of a small minority. Rather, I am suggesting that the widespread presence of such goods in British shops and thus the imagined possibility of purchase transforms the symbolic meaning of Hollywood stars from distant objects of desire from another world to more familiar and everyday signs of femininity replicable through consumption. (Stacey, 1994: 240)

It is not hard to recognise this in the current trend in women's magazines, television lifestyle and makeover programmes, and online, to provide guides on where to buy either the exact garment worn by the pictured celebrity or its cheaper substitute. Nor is it hard to see within this formation the seeds for the contemporary mobilisation of celebrity as a key location for the construction of cultural identity.

While the study is then quite resonant in what it can offer contemporary understandings of the consumption of celebrity, Stacey is careful to discriminate in terms of the historical moment as well as the geographic location of the audiences. The cultural processes in play are both contingent and determinate, not merely the inevitable consequence of textual forms or promotional practices. What Stacey describes is a relational shift; as the distance between her respondents and the stars diminishes, the relevant discursive frame moves from escape to identification. Even as she (persuasively) describes this shift, however, she is careful not to fall into the trap set by 1970s screen theory of essentialising spectatorship. The detailed historical research that has gone into developing her explanation of this shift, she says, should not be allowed to erase the 'complexities of the multiple meanings of female spectatorship' (ibid.: 239). What emerges is an exemplary study of the complex and multiple mediated uses to which the film star is put by an audience fraction at a particular time and in a particular location. As such, it is a model of what kind of work might be done in relation to the contemporary situation by researchers within cultural studies if we are to better understand the contemporary consumption of celebrity.

CONSUMING CELEBRITY ONLINE

As we have seen, the expansion of the presence of celebrity online and over social media has transformed both the production and the consumption of celebrity over the last decade. There is now a plethora of outlets for celebrity content online – blogs, news bulletin boards, and official celebrity sites, as well as the online presence for news media from all other platforms. There is also a wide range of modes of interaction, through which the consumption of celebrity can occur – to the point of enabling the generation of new, reme-diated, celebrity content that in turn migrates onto official sites, Twitter feeds, and even the evening news. We have so far talked about modes of consumption that are largely productive, playing positive roles in the con-struction of community and identity. We have also encountered arguments, on the other hand, that even the positive consumption of celebrity may carry its dangers; the 'celebrity worship' paradigm is, in my view, the least persua-sive version of this. In this last section of the chapter, I want to consider the consumption of celebrity online in ways that arguably more accurately reflect the dominant modes of consumption, and that also demonstrate how little 'celebrity worship' may be actually going on when most people deal with the representation of celebrity online.

Amongst many of the most high profile celebrity gossip sites – Perez Hilton, Oh No They Didn't (ONTD), The Superficial, for instance – there is plenty of material that replicates the kinds of media treatment we discussed in relation to the celebrity magazines. There are the gushing and adulatory accounts of celebrity performances: so, ('Queen Bey') Beyonce's performance of the national anthem at Barack Obama's second inauguration in 2013 is described on Perez Hilton's blog as 'amazing' and a 'must-see'. But there is also the famil-iar skepticism and cynicism: a day later, then, the headline on Perez Hilton accuses Beyonce of lip-syncing her performance. Even in those sites which depend upon fans hungry for celebrity gossip, there is a readiness to shift from admiration to antagonism without any sense of inconsistency. This is a long way from celebrity worship. Indeed, there is a slightly corrosive tendency for gratuitous attacks on celebrities that treats them as fair game for whatever kind of treatment might amuse the online fan. So, the gossip website ONTD, a relatively benign location for celebrity gossip, has a photo gallery entitled the 15 Ugliest Celebrity Feet (http://ohnotheydidnt.livejournal.com/70835054. html). Here, fans are able to see that Oprah, Iman and Naomi Campbell all appear to have bunions!

There are plenty of sites, however, which are nastier than that; Amy Watkins Fisher's highly critical discussion of the blogosphere's, and in par-ticular Perez Hilton's, treatment of Britney Spears describes them in this way:

> Bloggers like Hilton posit a 'no holds barred' take on celebrity culture that has found a lucrative commercial formula in lashing out at celebrities, spectacular-izing the reversal of the treatment of the star as beyond the realm of the mere mortal to popularize an Industry of Mean. His blog archives the pleasure he

visibly takes in recasting celebrity in a negative relation instead of a positive, privileging the bad over the good, the minor car accident over the academy award, the Sunday afternoon fashion misstep over the red carpet entrance. (Fisher, 2011: 317).

As the fan comment quoted in the title of Fisher's article suggests ('we just love this train wreck'), notwithstanding its inherent mean-spiritedness, this has proven a rich vein of consumer interest to mine. As Johansson (2006) argues, celebrity-bashing stories link in with wider issues to do with class and identity, as the consumer exercises a pleasing sense of power and control over the privileged. There is also a gender dimension to this as the misfortunes of female celebrities have moved further into the foreground of public attention in recent times. A great many of these 'train wrecks' are women. In their introduction to what is the first volume of work devoted to examining the female celebrity so far, Holmes and Negra argue that 'one reason why stories of professionally accomplished/personally troubled female celebrities circulate so actively, is that when women struggle or fail, their actions are seen to constitute "proof" that for women the "work–life balance" is really an impossible one' (2011: 2). Furthermore, they point to the conservative and gendered 'pleasures of identifying and judging' the behaviour of 'out-of bounds' women (ibid.: 2). There are some significant structural, socio-political, reasons for the market for the celebrity-bashing story, it would seem. These, however, still don't seem enough to explain the 'hysterical' tone of these stories (which is how Fisher [2011: 317–8], I think accurately, describes Perez Hilton's 'open letter to Britney' from 2007), nor the tone of self-righteousness that accompanies so much of what Fisher describes as 'tabloid bottom-feeding' (ibid.: 316). Unlike the mix of enthusiasm and criticism that Andrejevic (2008) finds in TelevisionWithoutPity, a site (and television show) such as *TMZ* seems to be uncomplicatedly predatory in its practice and objectives. *TMZ* generates the 'gotcha' moment on a regular basis in a way that reminds one of the late *News of the World*: it was *TMZ* that brought us the most disturbing images of Britney Spears' personal unraveling (the late night shopping expeditions without underwear, the head shaving and so on), as well as Prince Harry's naked romp in a Las Vegas hotel room. In both of these cases, *TMZ* was able to translate this material into major stories for mainstream news outlets and thus was happy to claim to be serving the public interest in the manner of traditional journalism.

Speaking from outside the target market concerned, it is hard to admire what occurs at this end of the production and consumption of celebrity online. Even when consumed in the playful manner suggested in the first part of this chapter, one has to accept that the pleasures of this kind of celebrity material are derived from their capacity to be invasive, exploitative and vengeful. It may not, however, represent the nadir of the ways in which celebrity is experienced online. For that, we need to enter the territory of 'celebrity flesh', the naked celebrity. The specific modes of consumption I want to highlight in relation to this kind of content may well operate in ways that are difficult to interpret from the outside, appearing to run against the grain of the practices we have been examining so far in this chapter. Nevertheless, this kind of material – linking as it does to soft pornography sites – does constitute one end of the range of consumption practices currently in play and thus demand attention. Ultimately, I would contend, the practices I examine here take us beyond the specific contexts of production within which I have situated celebrity for this book, emphasising the mobility of celebrity and its availability for appropriation into other domains of commodification and consumption.

There are precursors for the nude celebrity sites in the basement market celebrity magazine which prints nude celebrity shots, some gossip, movie reviews and, in some cases, amateur nude shots sent in by readers of the magazine. The inside front page of an issue of the Australian-based nude celebrity magazine, *Celebrity Flesh*,[8] carries a manifesto. Headed, 'Fuck Me I'm Famous', it celebrates its difference from 'trashy magazines' about stars 'NOT WEARING ANY MAKE-UP (argh!) or CAUGHT WEARING SHABBY CLOTHES (nooo) or OUT WITH A BAD HAIRDO':

> No, this is about tits-out, daks-down, anus-in-your-face famousness. Eewww!
>
> *Celebrity Flesh* goes to the heart of what celebrity is all about – nice faces and naked cunts, cocks, tits and arses.
>
> Let's face it, they're the CORE attraction. Everything else is just window dressing – the fashion, the cabbage diets, the royal weddings, the funerals, the drugs, the puppies, the babies and the Peruvian tribal rugs spun by third world child labourers high on glue …
>
> But, of all magazines, *Celebrity Flesh* comes closest to that SEARING TRUTH because we, at least, get to first base, to wit, NAKEDNESS.
>
> And it's a proud tradition we've been following since 1999, so we know what we're doing. We're professionals. (Anonymous, 2002: No.3, p. 2)

Self-mocking and cynically media-savvy, the claims it makes about 'the searing truth' of celebrity are, of course, meant to be comically hyperbolic. Nonetheless, the manifesto and the content of the magazine it introduces constitute an aggressive attack on conventional celebrity gossip as so much trivial fooling about. Celebrity, here, is defined in an exclusivist and objectifying manner: happily provocative and deliberately offensive, the manifesto leaves little room for the things focused upon in this book so far (the construction of community, for instance). Celebrity is the spectacle of a particular kind of sexual objectification, and that's all.

Such an attitude is largely carried over into the online nude celebrity sites that have been proliferating since the late 1990s. Usually demanding that viewers subscribe before accessing the sites' content, much in the way standard porn sites work, these websites offer the opportunity of seeing their favourite stars naked. Most of the images displayed are provided through paparazzi shots, through stills or video captures from movies, or lifted from photo-spreads in more reputable or mainstream magazines like *FHM*, *Vanity Fair* or *Playboy*. None of it is generated independently by the website itself. The exception to this rule is the fake – that is, the face of a famous person is placed on the naked body of someone else. This is so prevalent that there are now sections in both kinds of outlet that cater to an interest in the quality of the illusion created and suggest that the point of the exercise is the spectacle of disrespect rather than finding out 'what they are really like'. Interestingly, then, it is not so much the pictures themselves – because so many of them will circulate through other means elsewhere as well – as the framing discourses that differentiate these sites, and the magazines which preceded them, from other parts of the celebrity industry.

In the vast majority of the sites I have seen, the displays of naked celebrities are accompanied by a similar discourse to that used in the *Celebrity Flesh* manifesto: cheery, enthusiastic, unrepentant, and confident that the interests of the consumers they serve have as much to do with soft-core pornography as with celebrity. What celebrity provides through these websites is a point of entry, effectively, to another industry. This is demonstrated by the shifts in content as you move through the celebrity websites. The official or institutional celebrity website is often only one click away from a link to the 'hot' or 'sexy' pictures. This site, too, may still be relatively respectable in its framing discourses, but the chain of further links promising even sexier revelations is intended to discourage the visitor from stopping there. The ideological journey on offer is legible through the names of the sites. Representative of the soft-porn/mainstream variety of image is a site called *Celebrity.Wonder.com*. Here the emphasis is as much upon glamour as revelation, and therefore its interests are not entirely discontinuous with the celebrity industries we discussed in Chapter 2 – notwithstanding the site's slight preference for nude or topless pictures. Similarly, the range of videos available through online video sites such as *metacafe* address this kind of demand as well: while satisfying an interest in the star, the celebrity or the particular textual vehicle (the movie or TV show), it also provides excerpted sex scenes and compilations of sex scenes from mainstream movies or television programmes in which the star of your choice is performing. However, the pursuit of more explicit images or performances of the chosen star can take the visitor to, for example, a site called *Hollywood Whores*. The revelations offered here refer to a different 'reality' behind the stars – their underlying availability as objects of sexual display – and they are framed in an unapologetically and unmistakably misogynistic manner. In this domain, the distance between regarding celebrities with wonder to regarding them as whores is surprisingly short, but the kinds of images available in the latter context are significantly different. Fakes proliferate and are accompanied by bogus sex videos involving Britney Spears or Eva Mendes as well as the ubiquitous Pamela Anderson–Tommy Lee video. At this end of the chain, the links are no longer to other celebrity sites but only to porn sites.

Clearly, a site such as *Hollywood Whores* operates without the consent of those whose images are displayed. Consequently, even though the sites and the nude celebrity magazines occupy one end of the range of representational practices concerned with the promotion of celebrity, it is probably legitimate to say that they do not operate in the interests of the celebrity industry in anything other than a peripheral way. Instead, the sites in particular provide a means of attracting a market for the pornography industry, as it simply siphons off visitors from the more anodyne sites. It is important to emphasise that this is different, for example, from the way mass-market women's magazines might use celebrities to sell their products. The women's magazines sell celebrity as one of their core genres of content, whereas the porn sites use celebrity content as a means of attracting consumers who are then offered something else instead or as well. Alternatively, this practice may seem similar to the commercial practice of celebrity endorsement that uses the famous image to attract buyers of another product. The crucial difference in regard to the porn-celebrity sites is that theirs is not a consensual, contractual, arrangement benefiting both parties; the celebrity image is appropriated for uses to which many of those depicted would object.

Nevertheless, and with all of this understood, we need to accept that at least the initial interest satisfied by the nude celebrity sites and magazines constitutes one of the standard practices of the cultural consumption of celebrity. The desire to see what the celebrity is 'really like' obviously has a substantial sexual dimension and it is important to stress that this is more than satisfied by the many nude celebrity formats as well as by the more mainstream products of the celebrity industry without much interpellation of the discourses of pornography. That the visitor to the nude celebrity website is easily encouraged to explore further tells us that not only is there a commercial reason for this facility but also that it reflects an implicit tendency on behalf of at least some consumers. It is worth thinking about what might constitute the celebrity-based appeal here. As I argued in relation to the appeal of Diana in the previous chapter, the availability of the celebrity as a commodity and as an object of desire must not be overlooked as a fundamental component of their attraction. The nude celebrity magazines and sites exploit this to the hilt, offering the ultimate sign of availability – the unlicensed display of their naked bodies.

There is a further element to this. Some sites express the form of gendered anger or misogyny (explicit in the *Hollywood Whores* address, for instance) that Holmes and Negra (2011) describe. It is likely that the motivation of revenge we discussed earlier in a different context may be enacted here: in some cases the images displayed are a form of humiliation visited upon these high profile women. When we discussed such motives earlier on, however, it was in the context of a class-based sense of exclusion, a response to privilege. One of the modes of consumption I am describing may have a class-based, deliberately 'vulgar' discourse organising it, and the 'we're professionals' comment in the *Celebrity Flesh* manifesto does signify an ironic awareness of the constructedness of this discourse. At first glance, though, the objectives of these media products have more to do with revenge upon women than upon class privilege or power. However, I am also mindful of the kind of argument Laura Kipnis has made about the dangers of editing class out of post-feminist understandings of such representations. In her discussion of *Hustler* magazine, Kipnis (1992) argues against reading its images as the simple expression of misogyny – the tactic she says was routinely taken within academic feminism at the time she wrote her essay, and is one that still immediately offers itself when encountering such images. In relation to a *Hustler* feature that is directly relevant to our interests here, a notorious set of paparazzi photos of a nude Jackie Onassis, Kipnis suggests that it would be wrong to assume that Onassis was simply offered up to the reader as an image of the unwilling sexual object. Instead, it is also possible that she was presented as a political target. What Kipnis means is that there is a class dimension in play here, which motivates the humiliation these pictures generate, because Onassis clearly occupied a position that both symbolised and exercised class power and privilege. The opportunity available to the magazine was to undermine that power and this was most convincingly described as an expression of class resentment, Kipnis concludes, rather than as the expression of misogyny. My reading of these websites would suggest that both these possibilities are there.

As briefly noted in Chapter 3, with regard to the cam-girls phenomenon, the production of celebrity can spill over into other domains. In the cam-girls' case, too, the construction of DIY celebrity took them into porn portals and into relations with their visitors which, from some of the more critical points of view, approached those of sex workers. Consumption of celebrity is not sealed off from other cultural practices and the desires celebrity mobilises are not easily contained. I don't intend to embark on a more developed study of these related phenomena here, but we do need to acknowledge this end of the range of consumption practices. The practices we have been discussing are far from unproblematic and some way from the more mainstream practices and functions that were dealt with in relation to gossip earlier in this chapter. Nevertheless, they offer a reminder of the difficulty of providing an account of the cultural function of celebrity that will have equal explanatory power in all the contexts in which it arises. Simply, its pervasiveness has made it a highly extensive and contingent cultural discourse/commodity. As both Jackie Stacey's work and the sites in this section of the chapter demonstrate, in very different ways, making sense of the politics implicated in consuming celebrity at any one point in time is always going to be a complicated, nuanced, and contextualised process.

NOTES

1   Joke Hermes provides a useful reminder of this in her discussion of women read-ers of gossip magazines, where her respondents insist on the relative insignifi-cance of their engagement with these magazines. Although media and cultural studies critics might think they know better and thus attribute political signifi-cance to such consumption practices nonetheless (and there are plenty of instances of that), I think it is worth heeding Hermes' advice that we should take seriously these women's honest assessment of their experience. As she puts it, provocatively, we need to accept the possibility that 'media use is not always meaningful' (1995: 15).
2   These were groups of three to eight people, and composed of 'middle range' celebrity watchers. Gamson defines these as people 'who consistently but casually paid attention to a range of celebrities and regularly read or watched celebrity-based publications or programmes (they watched variety talk shows once a week or more, for example, or read an entertainment magazine once a month or more)' (1994: 145).
3   By this term, he means that the celebrity has risen to prominence 'naturally' as a result of organic rather than professional or industrial processes.
4   To counter that, consider the kind of description that Gamson provides of the experience of standing in the crowd beside the red carpet at the Academy Awards. He stresses how irreverent the whole process is, how indiscriminate is the crowd's interest in individual celebrities. The spectators he describes are as much engaged in the social activity of identifying the star as in any personal obsession. Gamson suggests that 'visible celebrity-watching activities are focused on collective experience: watchers are connecting with each other through the "sport" of sighting, identifying and categorising celebrities, exchanging bits of

information, or through their common experience of and role in the spectacle' (1994: 132). The command metaphor is that of participants in a sport:

> The seating arrangement is drawn from sports: bleachers overlook the 'field' onto which celebrities arrive. The crowd's behaviours also ape sporting events. There is the rowdiness – the calling out to friends, boisterous joking, milling around, chatting with strangers, collective complaining chants. (1994: 134)

5 I am indebted to Chris Moore's paper, 'I'm kind of a big deal on the Internet: Reddit.com and the reshaping of celebrity' (Celebrity Studies conference at Deakin University, December, 2012), for bringing this to my attention.
6 It is significant, in relation to our discussion of the death of Diana in the previous chapter, that such a point could be made. The fact that things did so dramatically fall apart, rather than continuing to provide us with soap opera entertainment, was among the aspects of her death that made it so shocking.
7 I am grateful to Alan McKee for pointing out that there is an exception to this argument about role models. For particular fractions of the community – gays, people with disabilities, people of colour – it may be more correct to recognise that certain high profile representatives of their group will operate as role models, as aspirational examples to be emulated. This is because these are groups who do not appear in the media as positive examples very often.
8 There are versions of this format elsewhere. Examples in the UK have included *Adult Sport* or *Celebrity Adult Spy*.

7 Conclusion: Celebrity and Public Culture

[S]ome have made [the] case ... that celebrity culture is an essential component of public debate about the issues that require public resolution, whether as part of an increasing personalization of politics ... or as part of a broader narrativization of democracy that includes a wider section of the public ... This contradicts a longer negative tradition which sees celebrities and the mediated events constructed around them, as pseudo-personalities and pseudo-events ... But such is the proliferation of celebrity culture ... that it can no longer simply be dismissed as external to the world of public issues.

(Couldry and Markham, 2007: 404)

TAKING CELEBRITY SERIOUSLY

One of the inevitable consequences of undertaking academic work on celebrity is being asked repeatedly – by journalists, by one's colleagues, sometimes even by taxi-drivers – why you would do such a thing. Celebrity, notwithstanding its exorbitant presence within our public culture, is widely dismissed as fundamentally trivial, ephemeral, or inconsequential. Nonetheless, and as I hope this book will have helped to establish, it is important that scholars in media and cultural studies recognise the need to take celebrity seriously. I want to spend a little time at the beginning of this concluding chapter on providing some of the reasons why this is so.

The production and consumption of celebrity plays a fundamental role in two of the key developments in the relation between the media, society and culture over the last two decades. The first is what has been described as the 'mediatisation'[1] of culture and society (Hepp, 2013) – that is, the sense that the media are now playing a more fundamental shaping role in our experience of everyday life. If the media, as Couldry (2003) suggests, are functioning as the 'social centre', then it may no longer be appropriate to see them as simply mediating between other important social actors – the government, industry, education institutions and so on. Rather, and there is much debate about all of this so I am simplifying dramatically here, many would argue that it now takes a leading and independent role.

The result is a situation where our lived experience of politics, culture and society has become increasingly 'moulded' (Hepp, 2013: 2) by the media. In its participation in the process of 'moulding' our culture, and as Couldry (2003) has explained, celebrity has served as a discursive, and for some an actual, bridge between the social centre of the media and the everyday life of 'ordinary people'; in this way it has contributed significantly to this process of mediatisation.

The second development is to do with how the media have responded to this reconfiguration of their role by consolidating their market power. This has occurred in a context of massively increased commercial competition as outlets proliferate and audiences choose from ever-expanding menus of content. Where once the media might have situated themselves as operating across the entertainment and information sectors, as well as across the commercial and the public sector, I have argued elsewhere (Turner, 2010) that they are now more definitively located within the entertainment industries; their information, and thus their public service, function is gradually receding in importance. Again, celebrity is significant in this repositioning of the media around the centrality of entertainment-based content. Indeed, celebrity has become a central structural component of the contemporary political economy of the media; take away celebrity and the industries which feed it, and some of the basic support systems for contemporary commercial media production go with them.

So, in both of these large-scale shifts – which have broad implications at a social and political level – celebrity, structurally embedded within the media industries as it is, plays a key role. There are also more specific tendencies to which celebrity contributes. If the media now play an increasingly important role in the production of cultural identities, as many have argued, then celebrity is a prominent participant in this process. We have discussed this at various points in this book already, but I want to re-emphasise two aspects of this participation here. Both of them move us away from any idea that the media simply represent cultural identities in order to provide models for emulation. As we have seen, it has never been this simple. However, P. David Marshall (2010) further complicates our understanding of this process when he describes the shift from a representational culture to a presentational culture, in which the production of identity is as much a personal performative practice as a mediated representational practice. Marshall uses the construction of the celebrity persona as a paradigmatic means of explaining that shift but, if he is correct, it affects more than just the construction of celebrity. Marshall's focus on social networks and the use of Twitter in particular is aimed at revealing the influence of the tools of celebrity on the presentation of the self at the level of the private life of the ordinary person. And when Skeggs and Wood (2012) interrogate the manner in which reality TV celebrities participate in the construction of certain kinds of public personhood, or when my own work (Turner, 2010) has also discussed the social consequences of privileging certain kinds of cultural identities through the performance of participants in reality TV programmes, we are not simply talking about a media representation. Instead, we are highlighting what Jack Bratich (2007) has described as the way reality TV works more like an 'intervention' into the social than a representation:

> [Reality TV] is a constituting technology – according to Jack Bratich (2007), it does not '*represent* the current conjuncture – it interjects itself into the conjuncture and enhances particular components required by it' ... [Like documentary] it does not just work at the level of the constative (representative) but also at the level of the performance through 'acts' which intervene in the social world. (Skeggs and Wood, 2012: 38)

Here, celebrity is not a field of representation to which we might respond as if to a body of texts; rather, it is a mode of intervention into the social which must be understood in terms that acknowledge the nature of its participation in the production of everyday life.

Another area where the rise of celebrity content accompanies a particularly significant shift in the definition and function of an aspect of the media is in relation to the current state of journalism. A sense of crisis in journalism has now been around for quite some time, predating the rise of digital media, and closely tied (as we saw in Chapter 4) to debates about the conflict between the commercial entertainment-based imperatives exemplified by the tabloid, and the traditional democratic mission of an informing media. The current situation – one that has developed in response to changing market conditions (the increased competition for audiences, a shrinking workforce, accelerated news cycles, and the multiplication of platforms) – has resulted in a significant redefinition of the news as entertainment. This redefinition means that the public's access to information has, in effect, become a secondary consideration for much of the industry; not only that, however, but the ethical structures which might once have provided an element of trust in what information *is* provided through the profession are under serious threat. The most infamous recent example of this, of course, is the phone-hacking scandal in the UK, where *The News of the World*'s enthusiastic prosecution of its 'gotcha' mode of journalism reached its logical conclusion. The commercial importance of celebrity news is fundamental to this situation, and to the practices that enabled it to develop, as journalists disregarded ethical and legal constraints in order to be the first to get to the 'private' story behind the prominent public persona. Many of these personae were, of course, celebrities and thus regarded – by the media and even by many of the public – as fair game. However, what seems to have turned the public against this media practice was not its treatment of celebrities but its deployment against ordinary citizens, in this case, the traumatised parents of a missing child.

We have discussed the effects of tabloidisation earlier on, of course, but it is certainly worth thinking further about what happens when these ethical orientations lose their purchase and, as a result, how comprehensively available celebrity becomes as a focus for media stories. In late 2012, an Australian radio programme which specialises in airing prank calls managed to make a successful call to the London hospital in which the Duchess of Cambridge was being treated for extreme morning sickness. They got through to medical staff by pretending, not very skilfully but nonetheless effectively, that they were Queen Elizabeth and Prince Philip. Once the call was broadcast – which occurred without the permission of the nurse who took the call – it became international news. The initial amusement at the success of the hoax call was transformed into dismay when the nurse in question took her own life – as a consequence, it was widely suggested, of the humiliation caused by the media coverage. Those sections of the media which had not been directly involved in the prank call immediately expressed their outrage at the programme's irresponsibility, igniting another media frenzy and putting the radio hosts into the spotlight as the culprits who were, it was implied, responsible for the woman's suicide. The hosts apologised in a long and tearful interview, but were still threatened with manslaughter charges (which did not eventuate). This, in turn, sent the radio hosts into counselling and ushered in another round of the media working out which bits of their own industry were most to blame. Without going into the ethics of the prank call as a practice, it is important to realise that the media are implicated in all kinds of contradictory ways in this story: they produced the prank call which was aired without permission and grossly breached the privacy of a prominent person; they then pursued the nurse responsible in order to fill out the story, camping outside her house for days and thus invading *her* privacy; when the media exposure appeared to have caused her to commit suicide, those who had hounded her for a story then turned on the original culprits, the radio hosts, in order to exact retribution from them. No matter which way the responsibilities were inflected, there was always a story to be told and someone to blame. Despite the vigorous moralism that framed each story, the opportunistic agility with which media outlets moved from one moral target to another demonstrated the fact that there was no underpinning principle of public responsibility in play here at all. Despite the constant claims for various pieces of the moral high ground, it is in fact the mere practice of engaging with celebrity journalism that provided each intervention with its justification.

After the events of 9/11 within the USA, we have been told, there seemed to have been something of an ethical backlash against the diet of celebrity and infotainment being fed to the US public as news. September 11, and the manner in which it was covered by the media in general, had graphically demonstrated what 'real' news looked like. Furthermore, the manner of its consumption provided an equally graphic demonstration of what modes of engagement real news demanded from its audiences. Set against this, the entertainment-based news content of the 1990s looked a little threadbare. According to US media reports at the time, circulations for celebrity magazines declined, celebrity-based talk-shows appeared to lose their relevance, and the raft of hybrid reality-celebrity television formats lined up for the next season was drastically culled. The trend towards reality TV which exploited the spectacle of humiliation or fear (formats such as *Fear Factor*, for instance) was put on hold as audiences demanded a little more responsibility and sensitivity from their networks. To what extent such a shift was itself a media beat-up, who knows? The likelihood that it did exist was sufficient to generate significant debates within the academy, particularly around the implications of September 11 for contemporary journalism. Zelizer and Allan's (2002) edited collection used the event as an occasion for close analysis of the ethical and public interest performance of contemporary journalism. We have already encountered analyses of this kind in this book, such as James Carey's (2002) attack on the delivery of the news into the clutches of the entertainment industry quoted in Chapter 4. Zelizer and Allan's focus is on journalism rather than celebrity, but through its interrogation of what September 11 might teach us about contemporary journalism it responds thoughtfully and usefully to the longer-term shifts that I have been suggesting are implicated in the contemporary production and consumption of celebrity.

If there was a shift in public sensibility engendered by the events of September 11, then it didn't last. The previously dominant fashions in infotainment news content regained their momentum, *Fear Factor* went ahead, and celebrity now plays an even more prominent a role in the media diets of US consumers than it did before (although newsstand sales for the celebrity magazines are showing significant signs of decline). Outside the USA, there wasn't even a blip in media practice and the public culture I have been describing continued on the trajectory I have outlined.

Notwithstanding the critical account I have just given, I need to reiterate that the available points of view on the usefulness and function of that public culture vary considerably. We have encountered those who celebrate what they regard as the reclaiming of a degree of popular sovereignty over media content, as well as those who bitterly condemn the diminution of the media's importance as the provider of information to the citizenry. The contemporary significance of celebrity for cultural and media studies is implicit in the fact that celebrity has continued to be a key battleground for debates about the social and political function, and the democratic potential, of our public culture. This remains the case, despite the fact that there continue to be many events – for instance, the Arab Spring – which remind us of the purpose of an earlier paradigm of news which still exists, awaiting re-activation from time to time.

It is not surprising that there are competing views and ambivalent attitudes towards such a situation. What I have been describing throughout this book is a phenomenon that requires a continual balancing act: between the need to properly understand the function of (especially) denigrated aspects of popular culture and the complacent politics that threatens to be among the products of such an understanding. The analysis of the productive cultural functions of celebrity – the 'identity work' it helps us to perform, for instance – must not obscure the equal importance of competing concerns. These might range from issues of privacy and redress for the subjects of 'attack dog' journalism, to the news media's diminishing capacity to perform the critical investigative work once regarded as its most fundamental democratic service.

Perhaps our judgements are least ambivalent when the discursive regimes and industrial processes of the celebrity-as-commodity migrate into other domains as a means of managing public perceptions of participants within those domains, and of determining the precise nature of the range of meanings in play. Publicity and public relations may play a routine and legitimate role in the entertainment industry and therefore their employment there may raise few political or social concerns. There are concerns, though, when the techniques used to produce celebrity are employed to manage the news and public debate, and in particular to manage the representation of political figures. This latter aspect is located towards the outer edge of the pervasiveness of celebrity in my view, and therefore has not figured large in this book so far. That said, it is worthwhile, before closing this account, to briefly discuss the influence of celebrity on organised politics.

CELEBRITY, POLITICS AND 'SPIN'

We noted earlier in this book that the systems used to produce celebrity in the entertainment and sports industries are very similar to those now used to produce the public persona of the politician. The need for the successful politician to build a public face means that the conventions of celebrity must collude with those of party politics. As Gamson puts it, 'the production setting in which political figures come to public attention mimics, and sometimes borrows techniques directly from, entertainment celebrity ... Like entertainers, politicians are coached, handled, wardrobed, made up, carefully lit' (1994: 189). Gamson's short discussion of politics highlights these similarities by pointing to the central role played by publicists in 'building a conventional celebrity sell' in order to get a politician elected (ibid.: 186–9). Richard Schickel has examined this process in American politics, charting its participation in the election of a series of US presidents, namely Eisenhower, Kennedy, Carter, and finally Reagan. He argues that election campaigns are now simply 'a contest between personalities': 'the issues merely provide the occasion for testing the personal appeal of the contenders' (Schickel, 1985: 146). (The two elections that Barack Obama won provide good examples of this.) The widespread international trend towards presidential-style campaigns – even in systems that resemble the Westminster or party-based parliamentary systems – reinforces this concern.

As I implied earlier on, this is partly a story about the ubiquity of public relations, of the widespread commercial installation of an industrial mechanism for the managing of public perceptions through the media. The influence of the 'smiling professions' upon the practice of journalism – in news, as well as in entertainment or sports journalism – has been fundamental. But there are other components to this story as well. The shifts in the approach to politics through news and current affairs formats on television, as well as the treatment of political news in the mainstream print media, reflect an increasing focus on the personal, arguably to the detriment of issues-based, or more structural, approaches. As we saw in the discussion of tabloidisation in Chapter 4, such a focus is reflected in entertainment formats as well, and it is to these formats that much of the coverage of politics has migrated in recent years. The rise of gossip journalism and the talk show, for instance, as well as satiric news commentary programmes such as *The Daily Show* and *The Colbert Report*, has challenged traditional sources of news and thus influenced how the process of mass-mediated political presentation must be organised. We have already seen how the talk show has been re-purposed to serve the interests of publicity rather than those of the public. As the popularity of these entertainment-based formats has increased, the consumption of the more traditional news formats has declined – and in some demographics this has been dramatic. West and Orman's discussion of celebrity and politics is one of many to draw attention to these trends:

> National surveys indicate that around 10 per cent of Americans get information about national politics from late-night entertainment shows such as *The Tonight Show* starring Jay Leno and *Late Night with David Letterman*. For those under the age of thirty years old, the figure rises to nearly half. As the

network news has emphasised entertainment features and lifestyle stories at the expense of hard news, more and more Americans have turned to entertainment shows for political commentary. (2003: 100)

The trend has accelerated since then, particularly in response to the rise of blogs and the capacity of social networks to filter and aggregate personal selections of news, share preferred items, and invite comment. There are those who see this as leading to a form of 'cyber-balkanisation' as consumers construct their own narrow news diets (what Sunstein calls 'The Daily Me'); there is concern that their engagement with politics is increasingly driven by personal preferences and thus progressively abstracted from public policy agendas (Sunstein, 2009). It is now commonplace for media pundits and academics alike to point to the virtual absence of the younger demographics from television news audiences, to the steep decline in the numbers of young people who read newspapers, and to the gradual disengagement of this demographic (and particularly those who are avid consumers of celebrity) from conventional news journalism and traditional politics (Couldry and Markham, 2007; Inthorn and Street, 2011). It is a trend that has actively encouraged the merging of the interests of organised politics with the production processes of celebrity. This is not only a simple matter of selling the glamour or presence of the spectacular politician, or of seeking new ways of tailoring the political for a wider range of potential markets. It is also implicated in how the political culture manages the media's treatment of particular political issues and the media's access to information about them. This has excited vigorous debate, especially within the media themselves, about the operation of 'spin'.

The management of the media's reporting of politics has become increasingly important to contemporary political campaigns and the day-to-day administration of government. Public relations consultants, media advisers and press officers have proliferated in western political systems and have become standard components of the contemporary furniture of democratic administrations. Widely referred to these days as 'spin doctors', their tasks range from writing press releases to briefing legal teams on controlling information through court injunctions, judicial suppression orders and the like. Often trained as journalists, spin doctors are employed to serve the politician's and not the public's interest, and are understandably resented both by the media and by the public as anti-democratic functionaries who intervene between the public and their representatives.

Developed in symbiosis with the aggressive modes of reporting and newsgathering that some argue made it necessary (Greenslade, 2002), the adoption of the modes of media management described as spin is now widespread. This is hardly surprising. The rise of the publicity and public relations industries in other domains has demonstrated a capacity for media management that was always going to be irresistible to party machine politics. Closely articulated to the development of public opinion polling as a means of generating political news stories and tracking public perceptions, the management of public personae has become a core activity for contemporary politics. Politics is now overwhelmingly about the management of the media representation of individuals, of specific areas of debate, or of the party's 'message' of the moment. The strategies employed are overwhelmingly derived from, on the one hand, public relations' models of crisis management and, on the other hand, from the celebrity industry's methods for building the public identity of the celebrity-commodity. The motivations that govern their use are entirely aligned with protecting the interests of specific political entities. Unlike most other areas of the tabloidisation debates, the operation of spin has not elicited strong or principled arguments in defence of its practices. Greenslade (2002) has, it is true, argued that politics' embrace of a high level of media management only developed as a response to the media's own irresponsibility, and he has also reminded us that the defence of an individual politician's privacy and personal reputation against the excesses of contemporary journalism is indeed a legitimate public issue. Nonetheless, it is widely acknowledged that the spin doctor's mode of media management is intended to control the public's access to the information upon which a democratic politics depends. This is not necessarily accomplished simply by denying access, however; more often it is achieved through the diversion of the public's interest from a sensitive issue to something less contentious by the timing of the release of information or the promotion of other news agendas. One political journalist has called the spin doctors 'weapons of mass distraction' (Crawford, 2002: 2), highlighting their ability to control agendas and levels of visibility rather than actually suppress information.

This discussion has begun to move us away from the original departure point for this section of the chapter – the celebritisation of politics – and I want to return to this theme by addressing another aspect of that process. This is the incorporation of celebrities themselves into party politics, something that is highly developed in the United States. (One political analyst, quoted by Gamson, says the institutionalisation of personality-driven political manipulation is 'as American as apple pie' [1994: 189].) As a trend, it has accelerated over the last couple of decades and, according to West and Orman, 'the emerging pattern of celebrity politics' has 'transformed American politics':

> Prominent individuals use fame either to run for elective office or influence those who do. They are able to draw on their platform to raise money for

themselves and other politicians. In a media-centred political system, celebrities are adept at attracting press attention. They make great copy and reporters love to build stories around glamorous celebrities. (2003: 6)

As a result, celebrities have become 'integrally involved' in political activities: electioneering, fund-raising, lobbying and so on – not always successfully, I might add: think of Clint Eastwood's bizarre debate with an empty chair at the 2012 Republican convention. When it is successful, the pay-off for the celebrity is twofold: it contributes to their overall professional strategy of marketing their own celebrity-as-commodity, and it also gives them political influence within the party. This may even lead to the pursuit of political office, of course. The USA is used to seeing celebrities from the entertainment and sports industries running successfully for political office; the most high profile example in recent years was the election of Arnold Schwarzenegger as governor of California in 2003 but there have been many more.

To some outside the USA, such events may seem to belong to the category of the 'only in America' stories that routinely turn up in the news media of other countries. That would be far too superficial a response however. West and Orman explain the specificity of the political power of the celebrity in the US in this way:

Even though Americans tend not to trust politicians, they have greater respect for and confidence in celebrities who enter the world of politics … These individuals have a fame that transcends public service and a reputation for personal integrity. This allows them to succeed politically in ways that are unavailable to more conventional kinds of politicos. (2003: 102)

Far from rendering them suspect, such candidates' personal celebrity actually provides them with an ethical advantage over the politicians. If this is an accurate account, and I have no reason to doubt it, then the political role of the celebrity is clearly quite different in significant respects in the USA than in, say, the UK. (Although not at all unique: in the Philippines, for instance, there is a relatively common career trajectory which takes the entertainment celebrity into politics. Former actor Joseph Estrada was elected President in 1998.) West and Orman's book provides some surprises in this regard. For instance, their view on the integration of gossip journalism into the political domain is more positive than one would expect in other national contexts. They argue that the effect of Vietnam and Watergate on the American public's view of politicians has been to reinforce the need to expose public officials of all kinds to close scrutiny at a personal level. Given that the amount of personal scrutiny to which

Bill Clinton was subjected throughout his presidency will certainly have struck some non-Americans as surprising, such an argument has a great deal of explanatory power. The principle it describes is dramatically different from the unwritten rules surrounding the media reporting of politicians' personal lives in the UK, which effectively quarantines private behaviour from attention until it directly affects the politician's performance of his or her public duties.

In the contexts I know best, that of Australia and the UK, it is the fundamentally constitutive discourse of inauthenticity – always something to be negotiated by the celebrity-as-commodity – which constrains the political possibilities for the individual celebrity, and which makes running for political office seem more or less unthinkable. There are exceptions, of course – the actor Glenda Jackson comes to mind in the UK and the former lead singer for Midnight Oil, Peter Garrett, in Australia – but what I have been describing throughout as the ambiguous and ambivalent discursive formations within which celebrities must define themselves make it hard, simply, to take them seriously in this context. Again, in the contexts I know best, the danger for the politician who visibly 'celebritises' their self-representation is that they won't be taken seriously either. For the political system to embrace such a strategy of self-representation, then, would be to risk discrediting the whole enterprise altogether. It is this possibility that so concerns those who criticise what they see as the celebritising of politics. Furthermore, as I argued earlier, when such a process is used in order to subordinate the representation of the political issues to the celebritised persona of the politician, it is widely recognised that the capacity for public debate is diminished.

In Part Two of this book I argued that the commercial objective of the production arms of the celebrity industry was to achieve as much control as possible over media access to and representation of the celebrity-commodity. Alternatively, my examination of the consumption of celebrity in Part Three demonstrated how difficult it was routinely to achieve that objective in practice. Consequently, some of the examples of celebrity I have examined in this book have been articulated to something like a de-centring of media power. They have taken many forms – the eruptive celebrity offered to ordinary people by reality TV, for instance, or the DIY micro-celebrity online. What I described as the demotic turn in media content was explicitly disconnected from an intrinsically democratic politics, but it was seen to hold possibilities for the exercise of a greater degree of popular sovereignty over media content – and a greater degree of media access for ordinary people. Where I treated the consumption of celebrity as a potentially productive social activity it was because, through their consumption of the celebrity-commodity, the consumer accessed some forms of power. It seems to me that the incorporation of the techniques of celebrity management into organised politics is intended to neutralise the power vested in such modes of consumption. Instead, it serves to retrieve and concentrate power in the hands of an elite that controls certain aspects of mass media access and content in order to protect their own interests. The implications of this development, then, run against the grain of, and therefore must qualify, the arguments made about the productiveness of 'celebrity from below' in Chapter 5.

As I said at the beginning of this section, the celebritisation of politics does sit towards the outer edge of my conceptualisation of the working of celebrity in popular culture today. It certainly exploits aspects of the systems of celebrity production we have described and the mode of consumption it invites retains the capacity for the kinds of ambiguities and contradictions I noted elsewhere. We still actively interpret the representations of politics, no matter how well it is managed. However, unlike that involved in most of the productions of celebrity I have examined in this book, the work of the political spin doctor is primarily intended to interrupt public access to information. The entertainment industry publicist may need to do this occasionally as well, but their primary aim is to attract attention to a menu of preferred choices for cultural consumption. These are significantly different sets of priorities. From time to time – for instance, in the case of the legitimacy of the official justifications for the US-led attack on Iraq – access to political information is of extreme public importance. Impeding public access to that information is a media intervention of a very different order to that involved in massaging the image of Russell Brand or Tom Cruise. It demands attention in a far broader range of contexts than is available to us here and ultimately it takes us beyond the consideration of celebrity altogether.

CONCLUSION

Celebrity's pervasiveness – an attribute I have been emphasising throughout this book – makes the objective of writing a short book on the topic a difficult one to achieve. I cannot hope to have been entirely comprehensive in the range of contexts within which my arguments have been made. They have been chosen for their illustrative value, rather than as a means of mapping the full range of cultural contexts in which celebrity plays its part. However, I do hope to have been more successful in the range of approaches that I have canvassed. The division of the book into separate treatments of production and consumption has attempted, among other things, to recognise the different approaches needed to understand a cultural practice of this kind. Such a division emphasises the importance of understanding the industrial conditions that produce celebrity, in a context where so much of the published work in cultural and media studies has concentrated upon the analysis of celebrity – often, of individual celebrities – as texts. Textual approaches have given due regard to the spectacular nature of celebrity as a media product but are less concerned with understanding how these spectacles got there in the first place. It is one thing to notice the proliferation of sites that feature celebrity texts; it is another to understand the industrial and cultural shifts implicated in causing this. In cultural studies today we need to come at such things from as many angles as possible if we are to understand the multiplicity of significances they generate. It is pleasing to note that in the last five or six years we have seen an expansion in the range of approaches in play – for instance, there is a greater interest in mapping the constitution of celebrity at particular historical conjunctures (Inglis, 2010; Hindson, 2011) and through media-specific industrial practices (Bennett, 2011), as well as a welcome revival in interest in the gendered nature of celebrity and its consumption (Holmes and Negra, 2011).

In the discourses through which it is publicly circulated, celebrity is routinely treated as a domain of irrationality, its appeal explained through metaphors of magic (charisma) or pathology (delusion). While the purchase of such explanations is certainly part of the story of the workings of celebrity in western culture today, in this book I also wanted to demonstrate the value of additional, and perhaps more empirical, approaches to explaining its operation. Fundamental here was focusing upon those parts of the media industries that have so often been left out of academic accounts in this area – pre-eminently, the work of publicity and promotions. Approached from this perspective, both the ambiguities and the power of celebrity as a component of our public culture seem to me a little clearer. When we conceptualise celebrity as something to be professionally managed, as well as discursively deconstructed, we think about it differently. It is possible to understand how this is done, by examining work practices, the cultures of production and so on. Such approaches have become routine within accounts of other media products, such as the production of news or of television. They constitute a significant part of what I have tried to reflect in this book, demonstrating the usefulness of a multiperspectived set of approaches to such a cultural phenomenon.

Further, I have been concerned to discuss celebrity in the context of the continuing debates about the performance of the media within contemporary public culture – issues of tabloidisation, of entertainment versus information, democratainment and so on. There is no easy response to any of these, it seems to me. Cultural studies has enabled us to address them in a theorised and politically attuned manner, but it has also alerted us to the political contingencies involved. What emerges is that it is unhelpful to go for the global explanation while we still have the option of paying close attention to the specific power relations in play at particular historical conjunctures. We must continue to engage in explicit debates about the current performance of democratic ideals through the media; indeed, this seems to me a function to which cultural studies should re-commit itself. The lesson for me at the end of the process of writing this book is that these debates are not easily resolved if they are disconnected from their specific historical, cultural and industrial contexts. Celebrity has the potential to operate in ways that one might deplore or applaud, but neither potential is intrinsic. What I have tried to do in those chapters dealing with these issues is to give the various angles of inspection their due, as a means of exploring the problem further.

Nevertheless, even when approached from a number of angles, there will be much about celebrity we still don't know. I have explained celebrity as a number of things: as a discursive effect, as a commodity, as an industry, and maybe even as a form of social relations. I am ready, however, to accept that this may still not entirely explain the force of the celebrity-fan relation described by Jackie Stacey's correspondents. Nor the wonderful final paragraph in Richard Dyer's *Stars* where he reminds us that – for all his focus upon analysis and demystification – when he sees Marilyn Monroe he catches his breath (1979: 184). I want us to understand celebrity and I hope that this book will take us significantly further towards that objective, but it is important to keep such impulses in mind as among the reasons why we would want to do that, and why it will remain so difficult to achieve.

NOTE

1 There is an active debate about this term, and whether in fact we should be taking about 'mediation' rather than 'mediatization'; see Couldry (2012), Hepp (2013), and Livingstone (2009).

References

Alberoni, F. (1972) 'The powerless elite: Theory and sociological research on the phenomenon of stars', in D. McQuail (ed.), *Sociology of Mass Communications: Selected Readings*. Harmondsworth: Penguin. pp. 75–98.

Allen, K. (2011) 'Girls imagining careers in the limelight: Social class, gender and fantasies of "success"', in S. Holmes and D. Negra (eds), *In the Limelight and Under the Microscope: Forms and Functions of Female Celebrity*. New York and London: Continuum. pp.149–73.

Andrejevic, M. (2004) *Reality TV: The Work of Being Watched*. Lanham, MD: Rowman and Littlefield.

Andrejevic, M. (2008) 'Watching television without pity: The productivity of online fans', *Television and New Media*, 9(1): 24–46.

Andrews, D.L. and Jackson, S.J. (2001) (eds) *Sports Stars: The Cultural Politics of Sporting Celebrity.*, London and New York: Routledge.

Ang, I. (1985) *Watching Dallas: Soap Opera and the Melodramatic Imagination*. London: Methuen.

Anonymous (2002) 'Fuck Me, I'm Famous', *Celebrity Flesh,* 3, p.: 2.

Becker, K. (1992) 'Photojournalism and the Tabloid Press' , in P. Dahlgren and C. Sparks (eds), *Journalism and Popular Culture*. London: Sage.

Becker, K. (1998) 'The Diana Debate: Ritual', *Screen*, 39(3): 289–93.

Bennett, J. (2011) *Television Personalities: Stardom and the Small Screen*. London and New York: Routledge.

Billig, M. (1992) *Talking of the Royal Family*. London and New York: Routledge.

Bird, S.E. (2002) 'Taking it personally: Supermarket tabloids after September 11', in B. Zelitzer and S. Allan (eds), *Journalism after September 11*. London and New York: Routledge. pp. 141–59.

Bonner, F. (2003) *Ordinary Television: Analyzing Popular TV*. London: Sage.

Bonner, F. (2011) *Personality Presenters: Television's Intermediaries with Viewers*. Farnham: Ashgate.

Boorstin, D. (1971) *The Image: A Guide to Pseudo-Events in America*. New York: Atheneum. (Originally published in 1961 as *The Image or What Happened to the American Dream?*)

Bourdieu, P. (1990) *In Other Words: Essays Towards a Reflexive Sociology*. Oxford: Polity.

Bratich, J. (2007) 'Programming reality: Control societies, new subjects, powers of transformation', in D. Heller (ed.), *Makeover Television: Realities Remodeled*. London: I.B.Taurus. pp. 1–5.

Braudy, L. (1986) *The Frenzy of Renown: Fame and its History*. New York and Oxford: Oxford University Press.

Brauer, L. and Shields, V.R. (1999) 'Princess Diana's celebrity in freeze-frame: Reading the constructed image of Diana through photographs', *European Journal of Cultural Studies*, 2 (1): 5–25.

Bromley, M. and Cushion, S. (2002) 'Media fundamentalism: The immediate response of the UK national press to September 11', in B. Zelitzer and S. Allan (eds), *Journalism after September 11*. London and New York: Routledge. pp. 160–77.

Campbell, B. (1998) *Diana, Princess of Wales: How Sexual Politics Shook the Monarchy*. London: Women's Press.

Carey, J.W. (2002) 'American journalism on, before, and after September 11', in B. Zelitzer and S. Allan (eds), *Journalism after September 11*. London and New York: Routledge. pp. 71–90.

Cashmore, E. (2003) *Beckham*. Cambridge: Polity.

Chaney, D. (1993) *Fictions of Collective Life: Public Drama in Late Modern Culture*. London and New York: Routledge.

Chaney, D. (2001) 'The mediated monarchy', in D. Morley and K. Robins (eds), *British Cultural Studies: Geography, Nationality and Identity*. Oxford: Oxford University Press. pp. 207–20.

Cheung, C. (2000) 'A home on the web: Presentations of the self on personal home pages', in D. Gauntlett (ed.), *Web.Studies: Rewiring Media Studies for the Digital Age*. London: Arnold. pp. 43–51.

Conboy, M. (2002) *The Press and Popular Culture*. London: Sage.

Connell, I. (1992) 'Personalities in the popular media', in P. Dahlgren and C. Sparks (eds), *Journalism and Popular Culture*. London: Sage. pp. 64–85.

Couldry, N. (2000a) *Inside Culture: Re-Imagining the Method of Cultural Studies*. London: Sage.

Couldry, N. (2000b) *The Place of Media Power: Pilgrims and Witnesses of the Media Age*. London and New York: Routledge.

Couldry, N. (2001) 'Everyday royal celebrity', in D. Morley and K. Robins (eds), *British Cultural Studies: Geography, Nationality and Identity*. Oxford: Oxford University Press. pp. 221–34.

Couldry, N. (2003) *Media Rituals: A Critical Approach*. London and New York: Routledge.

Couldry, N. (2012) *Media, Society, World: Social Theory and Digital Media Practice*. Cambridge: Polity.

Couldry, N. and Markham, T. (2007) 'Celebrity culture and public connection: Bridge or chasm?', *International Journal of Cultural Studies*, 10(4): 403–22.

Cowen, T. (2000) *What Price Fame?* Cambridge, MA, and London: Harvard University Press.

Crawford, B. (2002) 'Editors battle the twin sins of secrecy and spin', *Media, The Australian*, 10–16 October, p. 3.

Dahlgren, P. and Sparks, C. (eds) (1992) *Journalism and Popular Culture*. London: Sage.

Dayan, D. and Katz, E. (1992) *Media Events: The Live Broadcasting of History*. Cambridge, MA: Harvard University Press.

De Cordova, R. (1990) *Picture Personalities: The Emergence of the Star System in America*. Urbana and Chicago: University of Illinois Press.

Donoghue, F. (1996) *The Fame Machine: Book Reviewing and Eighteenth Century Literary Careers*. Stanford: Stanford University Press.

Dovey, J. (2000) *Freakshow: First Person Media and Factual Television*. London: Pluto.

Dovey, J. (2002) 'Confession and the unbearable lightness of factual television', *Media International Australia Incorporating Culture and Policy*, No. 104: pp. 10–18.

Dyer, R. (1979) *Stars*. London: BFI. (Revised edition 1998, *Stars: New Edition* (with Paul McDonald), London: BFI.)

Dyer, R. (1986) *Heavenly Bodies: Film Stars and Society*. London: BFI/Macmillan.

Eckert, S. (1991) 'The Carole Lombard in Macy's window', in C. Gledhill (ed.), *Stardom: Industry of Desire*. London and New York: Routledge. pp. 30–39.

Elliott, A. (1999) *The Mourning of John Lennon*. Melbourne: Melbourne University Press.

Elton, B. (2001) *Dead Famous*. London: Bantam.

Fisher, A.W. (2011) 'We love this train-wreck: Sacrificing Britney to save America', in S. Holmes and D. Negra (eds), *In the Limelight and Under the Microscope: Forms and Functions of Female Celebrity*. New York and London: Continuum.

Fowles, J. (1992) *Starstruck: Celebrity Performers and the American Public*. Washington, DC, and London: Smithsonian Institution Press.

Franklin, B. (1997) *Newszak and News Media*. London: Edward Arnold.

Friend, T. (2002) 'They love you!', *The Observer Magazine*, 8 December, pp. 34–45.

Frow, J. (1998) 'Is Elvis a god? Cult, culture, questions of method', *International Journal of Cultural Studies*, 1(2): 197–210.

Gabler, N. (1995) *Walter Winchell: Gossip, Power and the Culture of Celebrity*. London: Picador.

Gamson, J. (1994) *Claims to Fame: Celebrity in Contemporary America*. Berkeley: University of California Press.

Gamson, J. (1998) *Freaks Talk Back: Tabloid Talk Shows and Sexual Nonconformity*. Chicago: University of Chicago Press.

Garber, M. (1995) *Vice Versa: Bisexuality and the Eroticism of Everyday Life*. New York: Simon and Schuster.

Gauntlett, D. (ed.) (2000) *Web.Studies: Rewiring Media Studies for the Digital Age*. London: Arnold.

Giles, D. (2000) *Illusions of Immortality: A Psychology of Fame and Celebrity*. London: Macmillan.

Gitlin, T. (1997) 'The anti-political populism of Cultural Studies', in M. Ferguson and P. Golding (eds), *Cultural Studies in Question*. London: Sage. pp. 25–38.

Gitlin, T. (2001) *Media Unlimited: How the Torrent of Images and Sounds Overwhelms Our Lives*. New York: Metropolitan Books.

Gledhill, C. (ed.) (1991) *Stardom: Industry of Desire*. London and New York: Routledge.

Gough-Yates, A. (2003) *Understanding Women's Magazines: Publishing, Markets and Readerships*. London and New York: Routledge.

Greenslade, R. (2002) 'Spin the beginning', *The Guardian: Media*, 24 June, pp. 2–3.

Hansen, M. (1991) *Babel and Babylon: Spectatorship in American Silent Film*. Cambridge, MA: Harvard University Press.

Harper, S. (2006) 'Madly famous: Narratives of mental illness in celebrity culture', in S. Holmes and S. Redmond (eds), *Framing Celebrity: New Directions in Celebrity Culture*. London and New York: Routledge.

Hartley, J. (1992) *The Politics of Pictures: The Creation of the Public in the Age of Popular Media*. London and New York: Routledge.

Hartley, J. (1996) *Popular Reality: Journalism, Modernity, Popular Culture*. London: Edward Arnold.

Hartley, J. (1999) *Uses of Television*. London and New York: Routledge.

Hartley J. (2008) *Television Truths*. Malden, MA: Blackwell.

Hartley, J. (2009) *The Uses of Digital Literacy*. St Lucia: University of Queensland Press.

Hartley, J. and Lumby, C. (2003) 'Working girls or drop dead gorgeous? Young girls in fashion and news', in K. Mallan and S. Pearce (eds), *Youth Cultures: Texts, Images and Identities*. Westport CT and London: Praeger. pp. 47–67.

Hay, J. and Ouellette, L. (2008) *Better Living Through Reality TV: Television and Post-Welfare Citizenship*, Malden, MA: Blackwell.

Hepp, A. (2013) *Cultures of Mediatization*, trans. K. Tribe, Cambridge: Polity.

Herman, E.S. and McChesney, R.W. (1997) *The Global Media: The New Missionaries of Corporate Capitalism*. London and Washington, DC: Cassell.

Hermes, J. (1995) *Reading Women's Magazines: An Analysis of Everyday Media Use*. Cambridge: Polity.

Hermes, J. (1999) 'Media figures in identity construction', in P. Alasuutari (ed.), *Rethinking the Media Audience: The New Agenda*. London: Sage. pp. 69–85.

Hesmondhalgh, D. (2013) *The Cultural Industries* (third edition). London: Sage.

Hill, A. (2002) '*Big Brother*: The real audience', *Television and New Media*, 3(3): 323–40.

Hill, A. (2007) *Restyling Factual TV: Audiences and News, Documentary and Reality Genres*. London: Routledge.

Hills, M. (2002) *Fan Cultures*. London: Routledge.

Hindman, M. (2009) *The Myth of Digital Democracy*. Princeton and Oxford: Princeton University Press.

Hindson, C. (2011) 'Mrs Langtry seems to be on the way to a fortune: The Jersey Lily and models of late nineteenth century fame', in S. Holmes and D. Negra (eds), *In the Limelight and Under the Microscope: Forms and Functions of Female Celebrity*. New York and London: Continuum.

Hobson, D. (1982) *Crossroads: The Drama of a Soap Opera*. London: Methuen.

Holmes, S. (2009) 'Jade's back and this time she's famous: Narratives of celebrity in the *Celebrity Big Brother* race row', *Entertainment and Sports Law Journal*, 7:1, xx–xxxvi.

Holmes, S. and Negra, D. (eds) (2011) *In the Limelight and Under the Microscope: Forms and Functions of Female Celebrity*. New York and London: Continuum.

Holmes, S. and Redmond, S. (eds) (2006) *Framing Celebrity: New Directions in Celebrity Culture*. London and New York: Routledge.

Hopkins, S. (2002) *Girl Heroes: The New Force in Popular Culture*. Sydney: Pluto.

Horrie, C. and Nathan, A. (1999) *Live TV: Tellybrats and Topless Darts – The Uncut Story of Tabloid Television*. London: Pocket.

Inglis. F. (2010) *A Short History of Celebrity*. Princeton: Princeton University Press

Inthorn, S. and Street, J. (2011) 'Simon Cowell for Prime Minister? Young citizens' attitudes towards celebrity politics', *Media, Culture and Society*, 33(3): 1–11.

Jeffreys, E. (2010) 'Accidental Celebrities: China's chastity heroines and charity', in L. Edwards and E. Jeffries (eds), *Celebrity in China*. Hong Kong: Hong Kong University Press.

Jenson, J. (1992) 'Fandom as pathology: The consequences of characterisation', in L. Lewis (ed.), *The Adoring Audience: Fan Culture and Popular Media*. London and New York: Routledge. pp. 9–29.

Johansson, S. (2006) '"Sometimes you wanna hate celebrities": Tabloid readers and celebrity coverage', in S. Holmes and S. Redmond (eds), *Framing Celebrity: New Directions in Celebrity Culture*. London and New York: Routledge.

Johnson, R. (1999) 'Exemplary differences: Mourning (and not mourning) a princess', in A. Kear and D.L. Steinberg (eds), *Mourning Diana: Nation, Culture and the Performance of Grief*. London and New York: Routledge. pp. 15–39.

Johnson-Woods, T. (2002) *Big Bother*. St Lucia: University of Queensland Press.

Kear, A. and Steinberg, D.L. (eds) (1999) *Mourning Diana: Nation, Culture and the Performance of Grief*. London and New York: Routledge.

Kelly, K. and McDonnell, E. (eds) (1999) *Stars Don't Stand Still in the Sky: Music and Myth*. London: Routledge.

Khurana, R. (2003) *Searching for a Corporate Saviour: The Irrational Quest for Charismatic CEOs*. Princeton and Oxford: Princeton University Press.

Kilborn, R.W. (1998) 'Shaping the real: Democratization and commodification in UK factual broadcasting', *European Journal of Communication*, 13(2): pp. 201–218.

King, B. (1991) 'Articulating stardom', in C. Gledhill (ed.), *Stardom: Industry of Desire*. London and New York: Routledge, pp. 167–82.

Kipnis, L. (1992) '(Male) desire and (female) disgust: Reading *Hustler*', in L. Grossberg, C. Nelson, and P. Treichler (eds), *Cultural Studies*. New York and London: Routledge. pp. 373–91.

Kitzmann, A. (1999) 'Watching the Web watch me: Explorations of the domestic web cam', MIT Communications Forum, http://web.mit.edu/comm-forum/papers/kitzmann.html#f17

Klein, N. (2000) *No Logo*. London: Flamingo.

Knee, A. (2006) 'Celebrity skins: The illicit textuality of the celebrity nude', in S. Holmes and S. Redmond (eds), *Framing Celebrity: New Directions in Celebrity Culture*. London and New York: Routledge.

Kuhn, A. (1998) 'Preface to Special Debate: Flowers and tears – The death of Diana, Princess of Wales', *Screen*, 39(1): 67–8.

Langer, J. (1981) 'Television's "personality system"', *Media, Culture and Society*, 3(1): 351–65.

Langer, J. (1998) *Tabloid Televison: Popular Journalism and the 'Other' News*. London: Routledge.

Leadbetter, C. (2000) *Living on Thin Air: The New Economy*. Harmondsworth: Penguin.

Leff, L.J. (1997) *Hemingway and His Conspirators: Hollywood, Scribners, and the Making of American Celebrity Culture*. Lanham, MD: Rowman and Littlefield.

Leppert, A. and Wilson, J. (2011) 'Living *The Hills* life: Lauren Conrad as reality star, soap opera heroine, and brand', in S. Holmes and D. Negra (eds), *In the Limelight and Under the Microscope: Forms and Functions of Female Celebrity*. New York and London: Continuum. pp. 261–79.

Levy, B. and Bonilla, D.M. (eds) (1999) *The Power of the Press: The Reference Shelf*. 71: 1, New York and Dublin: H.W. Wilson Co.

Lewis, L. (ed.) (1992) *The Adoring Audience: Fan Culture and Popular Media*. London and New York: Routledge.

Livingstone, S. (2009) 'On the mediation of everything', *Journal of Communication,* 59(1): 1–18.

Lumby, C. (1997) *Bad Girls: The Media, Sex and Feminism in the 90s.* Sydney: Allen and Unwin.

Lumby, C. (1999) *Gotcha: Life in a Tabloid World.* Sydney: Allen and Unwin.

Lumby, C. (2006) 'Doing it for themselves? Teenage girls, sexuality and fame', in S. Redmond and S. Holmes (eds), *Stardom and Celebrity: A Reader.* London: Sage. pp. 341–52.

Marcus, G. (1991) *Dead Elvis: A Chronicle of a Cultural Obsession.* New York: Doubleday.

Marshall, P.D. (1997) *Celebrity and Power: Fame in Contemporary Culture.* Minneapolis and London: University of Minnesota Press.

Marshall, P.D. (2000) 'The celebrity legacy of The Beatles', in I. Inglis (ed.), *The Beatles, Popular Music and Society: A Thousand Voices.* London: Macmillan. pp. 163–75.

Marshall, P.D. (ed.) (2006) *The Celebrity Culture Reader.* New York and London: Routledge.

Marshall, P.D. (2010) 'The promotion and presentation of the self: Celebrity as a marker of presentational media', *Celebrity Studies* 1(1): 35–48.

Marwick, A. and boyd, d. (2011) 'To see and be seen: Celebrity practice on Twitter', *Convergence,* 17(2): 139–58.

Masciarotte, G.-J. (1991) 'C'mon girl: Oprah Winfrey and the discourse of feminine talk', *Genders,* 11: 81–110.

McCutcheon, L., Lange, R. and Houran, J. (2002) 'Conceptualization and measurement of celebrity worship', *British Journal of Psychology,* 93(1): 67–87.

McCutcheon, L., Maltby, J., Houran, J. and Ashe, D. (2004) *Celebrity Worshippers: Inside the Minds of Stargazers.* Baltimore, MD: PublishAmerica.

McDonald, M.G. and Andrews, D.L. (2001) 'Michael Jordan: Corporate sport and postmodern celebrityhood', in D.L. Andrews and S.J. Jackson (eds), *Sports Stars: The Cultural Politics of Sporting Celebrity.* London and New York: Routledge. pp. 20–35.

McGuigan, J. (1992) *Cultural Populism.* London: Routledge.

McGuigan, J. (2000) 'British identity and "The People's Princess"', *The Sociological Review,* February, 1(48): 1–18.

McNamara, K. (2011) 'The paparazzi industry and new media: The evolving production and consumption of celebrity news and gossip websites', *International Journal of Cultural Studies,* 14(5): 515–30.

Mieszkowski, K. (2001) 'Candy from strangers', *Salon.com,* August, 13, http://archive.salon.com/tech/feature/2001/08/13/cam_girls/

Miller, T., Govil, N., McMurria, J. and Maxwell, R. (2001) *Global Hollywood.* London: BFI.

Milmo, C. and Akbar, A. (2002) 'BBC raises the stakes with new "reality TV" show', *The Independent,* 1 July, p. 5.

Monaco, J. (ed.) (1978) *Celebrity: The Media as Image Makers.* New York: Delta.

Moore, C. (2012) 'I'm kind of a big deal on the Internet: Reddit.com and the reshaping of celebrity'. Paper delivered to the Inaugural Celebrity Studies conference, Deakin University, December.

Moran, J. (2000) *Star Authors: Literary Celebrity in America.* London: Pluto.

Morgan, S. (2011) 'Celebrity: Academic "pseudo-event" or a useful concept for historians?', *Cultural and Social History,* 8(1): 95–114.

Morley, D. (1986) *Family Television: Cultural Power and Domestic Leisure.* London, Comedia.

Murray, S. (2003) 'Media convergence's third wave: content streaming', *Convergence: The Journal of Research into New Media Technologies,* 9(1): 8–22.

Pertierra, A.C. and Turner, G. (2013) *Locating Television: Zones of Consumption.* London and New York: Routledge.

Pieper, C. (2000) 'Use your illusion: Televised discourse on journalism ethics in the United States', *Social Semiotics,* 10(1): 61–79.

Redmond, S. and Holmes, S. (eds) (2006) *Stardom and Celebrity: A Reader.* London: Sage.

Rein, I., Kotler, P. and Stoller, M. (1997) *High Visibility: The Making and Marketing of Professionals into Celebrities.* Lincolnwood, IL: NTC Business Books.

Re:Public (Ien Ang, Ruth Barcan, Helen Grace, Elaine Lally and Justine Lloyd) (eds) (1997) *Planet Diana: Cultural Studies and Global Mourning.* University of Western Sydney: Research School in Intercommunal Studies.

Rodman, G.B. (1996) *Elvis After Elvis: The Posthumous Career of a Living Legend.* London and New York: Routledge.

Rojek, C. (2001) *Celebrity.* London: Reaktion.

Rojek, C. (2012) *Fame Attack: The Inflation of Celebrity and its Consequences.* London: Bloomsbury.

Roscoe, J. (2001) '*Big Brother* Australia: Performing the "real" twenty-four-seven', *International Journal of Cultural Studies,* 4(4): 473–88.

Rosen, J. (2006) 'The people formerly known as the audience', *PressThink: Ghost of Democracy in the Media Machine,* 27 June. http://archive.pressthink.org/2006/06/27/ppl_frmr.html (last accessed 24 January 2013).

Ross, A. (1989) *No Respect: Intellectuals and Popular Culture.* London and New York: Routledge.

Rowe, D. (1995) *Popular Cultures: Rock Music, Sport and the Politics of Pleasure.* London: Sage.

Sales, N.J. (2003) 'The camera wars', *Vanity Fair,* March, pp. 78–85.

Saltzman, J. (1999) 'Celebrity journalism, the public and Princess Diana', in B. Levy and D.M. Bonilla (eds), *The Power of the Press.* New York and Dublin: H.W. Wilson. pp. 73–5.

Scannell, P. (2002) '*Big Brother* as a Television Event', *Television and New Media,* 3(3): 271–282.

Scheeres, J. (2001) 'Girl model sites crossing line?' *Wired News,* 23 July, http//www.wired.com/news/ebiz/0,1272,45346.00.html

Schickel, R. (1985) *Intimate Strangers: The Culture of Celebrity in America.* Chicago, IL: Ivan R. Dee.

Schickel, R. (2000) *Intimate Strangers: The Culture of Celebrity in America* (revised edition). Chicago, IL: Ivan R. Dee.

Schmid, D. (2006) 'Idols of destruction: Celebrity and the serial killer', in S. Holmes and S. Redmond (eds), *Framing Celebrity: New Directions in Celebrity Culture.* London and New York: Routledge.

Senft, T.M. (2008) *Camgirls: Celebrity and Community in the Age of Social Media.* New York: Peter Lang.

Shattuc, J.M. (1997) *The Talking Cure: TV Talk Shows and Women*. New York and London: Routledge.

Shattuc, J.M. (1998) 'Go Ricki: Politics, perversion and pleasure in the 1990s', in C. Geraghty and D. Lusted (eds), *The Television Studies Book*. London: Edward Arnold. pp. 212–227.

Shepard, A.C. (1999) 'Celebrity journalists: It's part of Watergate's legacy: A highly paid, star-studded media elite. That's good for a handful of journalists, but is it good for journalism?', in B. Levy and D.M. Bonilla (eds), *The Power of the Press*. New York and Dublin: H.W. Wilson. pp. 79–87.

Silverstone, R. (1998) 'Special Debate. Flowers and tears: The Death of Diana, Princess of Wales: Space', *Screen*, 39 (1): 81–84.

Skeggs, B. and Wood, H. (2012) *Reacting to Reality Television: Performance, Audience and Value*. London and New York: Routledge.

Spigel, L. (2001) *Welcome to the Dreamhouse: Popular media and postwar suburbs*. Durham, NC: Duke University Press.

Stacey, J. (1994) *Star Gazing: Hollywood Cinema and Female Spectatorship*. London: Routledge.

Staiger, J. (1991) 'Seeing stars', in C. Gledhill (ed.), *Stardom: Industry of Desire*. London and New York: Routledge. pp. 3–16.

Storey, J. (2003) *Inventing Popular Culture: From Folklore to Globalization*. Malden, MA: Blackwell.

Sunstein, C. (2009) *Republic.com 2.0*. Princeton: Princeton University Press.

Taylor, A. (2013) 'Tweeting feminism: Naomi Wolf, celebrity and the (feminist) uses of social media'. Paper presented to *Console-ing Passions* conference, Leicester, UK, June.

Turner, G. (1999) 'Tabloidisation, journalism and the possibility of critique', *International Journal of Cultural Studies*, 2(1): 59–76.

Turner, G. (2001) 'Ethics, entertainment and the tabloid: The case of talkback radio in Australia', *Continuum*, 15(3): 349–358.

Turner, G. (2003) *British Cultural Studies: An Introduction* (third revised edition). London and New York: Routledge.

Turner, G. (2010) *Ordinary People and the Media: The Demotic Turn*. London: Sage.

Turner, G., Bonner, F. and P.D. Marshall (2000) *Fame Games: The Production of Celebrity in Australia*. Melbourne: Cambridge University Press.

van Krieken, R. (2012) *Celebrity Society*. London: Routledge.

Walker, A. (1970) *Stardom: The Hollywood Phenomenon*. London: Michael Joseph.

Wark, M. (1999) *Celebrities, Culture and Cyberspace: The Light on the Hill in a Postmodern World*. Sydney: Pluto.

Weinstein, D. (1999) 'Art versus commerce: Deconstructing a (useful) romantic illusion', in K. Kelly and E. McDonnell (eds), *Stars Don't Stand Still in the Sky: Music and Myth*. London: Routledge. pp. 56–71.

Wernick, A. (1991) *Promotional Culture: Advertising, Ideology and Symbolic Expression*. London: Sage.

West, D.M. and Orman, J. (2003) *Celebrity Politics*. Upper Saddle River, NJ: Prentice-Hall.

Whannel, G. (2002) *Media Sports Stars: Masculinities and Moralities*. London and New York: Routledge.

Whiteley, S. (2006) 'Celebrity: The killing fields of popular music', in S. Holmes and S. Redmond (eds), *Framing Celebrity: New Directions in Celebrity Culture*. London and New York: Routledge. pp. 329–42.

Wills, G. (1997) *John Wayne: The Politics of Celebrity*. London and Boston, MA: Faber and Faber.

Wilson, E. (1997) 'The unbearable lightness of Diana', *New Left Review*, No. 226, pp. 136–45.

Wood, H. and Skeggs, B. (eds) (2011) *Reality Television and Class*. London: Palgrave Macmillan.

Young, T. (2001) *How to Lose Friends and Alienate People*. London: Little, Brown.

Zelizer, B. and Allan, S. (eds) (2002) *Journalism after September 11*. London and New York: Routledge.

Index